To :

Christmas 2016.

The ATHENA Prodigies

Empowering Women Empowering Girls:

Stories and reflections to inspire you, to mentor her
and become prodigies of each other's wisdom
as you both pursue your dreams

By Danielle Joworski

Published by
Hasmark Publishing 1-888-402-0027
Copyright © 2015 by Danielle Joworski
First Edition, 2015

Cover Design and Photo: Monkey Peanut Creative Designs
(monkeypeanutcd@gmail.com)

Interior Book Design & Communications:
Profile Direct Marketing (www.profiledirect@qc.aira.com) &
Carolyn Flower Enterprises (www.carolynflower.com)

Author Photos: John Wills Photography (www.johnwillsphotography.com)

ISBN-13: 978-1-988071-08-4
ISBN-10: 1988071089

Endorsements

"Beautifully written and filled with inspirational stories. This book helps the reader find their light from within while empowering them to show our younger generation of woman that anything is possible"
Peggy McColl, New York Times Best Selling Author

"So many people fail to go after their dreams. Reading the stories in this book will inspire you to know it's possible to live the life of one's dreams. The section designed to assist younger woman and teens is an excellent resource for starting dialogue and life designing at an early age."
Sheena L. Smith, Dream Builder Coach-Licensed Brain Gym Instructor, Best Selling, Award Winning Author of "Life Simply Put"

"The ATHENA Prodigies in an excellent structure for all women and truly helps one draw out the power that is within! Being a success coach myself, I would say this book is an eye-opener for both mentors and mentees!"
Sonika Madarasmi Asif, Success Coach, Naveed & Sonika Coaching

"The ATHENA Prodigies is a must for all the brilliant women who wish to share their journey with aspiring young women who need to understand that the journey is where the learning occurs."
Sheila Trask, Personal Development Educator

Dedication

To my beautiful, budding children Alexander and Arabella,
I have never regretted leaving my career for you.
Thank you for your time, your help with this book and continually
letting me know that you love having your Mommy around.

Like we say at home …guess what? I love you!

To Steven, whose risk was larger than mine,
Your belief in me and support of my journey
to re-discover myself and identify
what I truly desire to be when I grow up is another
amazing story out of all of this.

Forward

I've known Danielle for 15 years and it seemed like every few years she would change what she was doing because she wasn't completely settled and happy with where she was going. She strived to move up the corporate ladder but in doing so she suffered on the inside because she was going after something she wasn't passionate about. How many people want to prove it to others, portraying one image on the outside but feeling completely different on the inside? I don't know the statistics of this but I bet it's pretty high, and I can speak from experience because I was one of those people.

Recently Danielle has inspired me in so many ways. I've seen her flourish becoming the women she has wanted to become and it all has to do with her following her dreams and her passion. She weathered her own storm, she did a lot of self-reflection, and got raw and real asking herself "what do I really want for me; for ME?"

Now, normally that sounds like a simple question but when you think deeply about this question it's something really hard to answer. Most people will go with the second best answer they come up with not striving for the true dream. You're the only one that can do this, nobody can do it for you and the reason for this is because you have to go on the inside, you have to ask yourself, are you sure of yourself? Do you have this feeling of confidence to go after what you really want? With Danielle's book she guides you in a way that is simple to understand yet very easy to implement in your life as a mentor and to help the mentee.

In our 'little life' we were able to use our imagination, and as we grew older it got clouded by a belief that's not very important to use anymore. This is something that this book will teach you to use again.

I feel very passionate about this book. This material will help women and children all over gain clarity on how to guide the mentor to help the mentee. You will be taught to breakdown your perceived barriers, carve out and established your own beliefs - your dreams.

Monica Da Maren
International best-selling author, Alone Together

The ATHENA Prodigies

Endorsements 3
Dedication 4
Forward 5-6
Introduction 8-9
Preface 10-20

Part I: Inspire Yourself and Discover Your Mentoring Talents...... 21
1 - Sharing this Book: Recommendations for the Mentor 22-23
2 - Storytelling, Reflecting & Mentoring as Learning Tools 25-31
3 - The Beginning: Tearing Down 31-34

Part II: For You - The Mentor 35
4 - Desires and Dreams 36-40
5 - Believing in Yourself 41-49
6 - Sticking to It ... You CAN Do it! 50-55
7 - Learning From Others 56-66
8 - Surrounding Yourself with the Best 67-80
9 - Making Decisions 81-87
10 - Listening to Yourself 88-98
11 - You Are Perfect 99-103

Part III: For Her - The Mentee 104
12 – Desires and Dreams 105-109
13 - Believing in Yourself 110-118
14 - Sticking to It ... You CAN Do it! 119-123
15 - Learning From Others 124-131
16 - Surrounding Yourself with the Best 132-145
17 - Making Decisions 146-154
18 - Listening to Yourself 155-161
19 - You Are Perfect 162-164

About the Author 165

Introduction

When starting to brainstorm how I wanted to tell my stories so that they could be shared with both women and girls, I initially struggled. Should I write one book or two? How could I tell my stories in a way that would relate to each reader and be age-appropriate? What should the title be so that I draw in my whole audience and let the world know that this is not your ordinary self-help book with one intended reader?

Once I made the decision to write one book but create separate sections in order to personalize the stories and knowledge to each individual reader, I began to reflect and collect the ideas and content from my own experiences and the feedback I had received from others over my almost 20-year career, my own children's experiences and stories from other caregivers. For my personal reflections and stories, they were written based on my perception of how I was reacting to situations at a given time. People, events and context have been altered to enhance the point of the learning opportunity that I am sharing so that the focus is on the lesson to be shared.

When thinking of a book title, I wanted it to possess the power and strength that we have as women and what we want for our young girls. I associated this desire to create empowered women to the Greek goddess ATHENA, known for her wisdom, strength and inspiration. As the book began to take root in providing learning opportunities for women and girls to develop powerful mentoring dyads , I saw my readers, women and girls, mentors and mentees, as being able to harvest and possess infinite knowledge from sharing and becoming prodigies of each other's wisdom.

This book is designed so that women and girls can start a dialogue, begin a conversation with themselves and each other to identify their dreams and desires that they really want. Each part of the book contains chapters that each deal with the same themes. **Parts I and II of the book are designated for just the mentor**, as an opportunity to reflect and learn about what you truly desire and sets you up to lead discussions with your mentee.

Part III of the book is designed for the mentor and mentee to work through together and builds on the strength and knowledge that the mentor has gained by reading her equivalent chapter in Part II. The learning opportunities provided for the mentee are told through stories and portrayed through the character "Samantha". Reflection questions are included at the end of each of the mentee's chapter for the mentor and mentee to answer together and start a dialogue, and sharing their knowledge.

Your experiences are unique to you and have made you into the wonderful person that you are. Each experience is a learning opportunity, made all the more powerful when others can learn from you.

The ATHENA Prodigies: Empowering Women Empowering Girls is about the growth, inspiration and empowerment of three entities; the mentor, the mentee and the mentoring dyad – it is unlimited construction of prodigies to the power of three! P3!

Preface

I believe that it is through the sharing of personal growth, achievements and battle scars that others can find inspiration.

We each have the capability to lead others and ourselves through precedent-setting journeys of self-discovery. By discovering the trove of talents you have, but may or may not be aware of, your ability to visualize and go after what you really want is possible. And having a positive perspective of yourself has the ability to attract positive experiences, enhancing your confidence and that of the others you choose to lead. You attract the vibrations you put out.

Be grateful for whom you are and the experiences you had to learn from. Learn to believe in yourself, to be true to yourself and to love who you really are. You and your dreams hold the key to unlocking your potential of accomplishing something extraordinary, and helping to mentor others to do the same.

Growing up, I would get a feeling that I was destined to do something great with my life. It was this feeling that drove me to work hard in high school and stuck with me throughout university, even as I struggled to find my path and myself. I had a thought, a burning desire, that I was going to be involved in something wonderful and unimaginable and that it was just over the horizon, a candle burning gently in the distance.

But after graduating from university and entering the professional world as a "career woman," the burning desire I used to feel that made me believe I was going to be spectacular fizzled out. I then turned into what I perceived to be a "normal career woman," following what I thought was the best path to success and trusting it was a path that would, at some point, lead to me feeling fulfilled. But after years of working, I found I was lost, helpless and overwhelmed with the burden I had placed on myself. It was a burden that eventually caused me to lose all sense of who I was.

My recovery from this state of mind began with a conversation, a seed that was planted and left to germinate deep into my subconscious for a few months. This seed of new belief was nourished and ideas from the seed began to grow like branches rooted in a growing belief that it was me who was actually in control of my life, not others. That if I was not happy, the ultimate power to change the direction of the path I had followed lay within me, and no one else -- that I actually held the key to unlocking the chains of self-doubt I had bound myself to.

I grasped onto this growing sense of self-belief and started to examine myself to identify who I was and what I needed to change in order to re-connect with the burning desire I once had -- that certainty that I was going to do something bigger than anything I had ever done before. As I did this, I gained confidence in myself again, and in the belief that I already knew what I needed to do.

I soon realized that, over the years, I had become a stranger to my family and myself. I further realized that there was absolutely no balance in my life, and that there had been none for a long time. The strain on my relationships with my children and husband were obvious and, when my children needed me, I was not there, or I was late, or I was too tired to nurture them in the way I wanted to. I identified myself as a woman who stood lonely and by herself, feeling that I did not know who I was.

I then made the decision to wage a war against the habits and paradigms that caused me to believe that the unsatisfactory life I was living was my only choice. I then changed my thinking into believing I could control and steer my life in the direction I wanted it to go in. And that if I took a moment to breathe and think about myself and what I wanted, what I really wanted, that the murky waters I was looking into would become clear and I would be able to forge a new life where I controlled the decisions and I was doing something I was passionate about. A life with a career that provided me with the balance I desired. Once I made that decision, I was steadfast in beginning to extrapolate a new path. I steadily turned into a woman who took an exponential risk in order to regain control of a situation I had been watching like a guilty bystander.

At the beginning of my journey, I felt like my story was nothing special and that I was not doing anything awe-inspiring. I was just, for the first time in many years, putting my family and myself first. What focused my mind on the route I needed to take in order to go after what I desired were the responses I received from women regarding the action that I took. My story is that I was an ordinary woman who took extraordinary efforts to best serve others first. My story started with growing up with self-esteem issues. Not feeling like I had close relationships as a child with family and friends definitely played a role in limiting the growth of my self-esteem. And growing up in a time when "boys were boys" and "girls were girls" definitely did not nurture what was to foreshadow my girl-power/millennium-women instincts that would show themselves every once in a while anyway (and which I am now embracing and having a lot of fun with).

My story is that I made the decision to retire from a lifestyle that was wreaking havoc on my life.

I resigned with no job to go to, only time with my family and myself, which was exactly what we all needed. And I got a lot of feedback about this decision which utterly amazed me. After I resigned, women began to seek me out. On one hand they could not believe that I was saying good-bye to my career, but they could believe and empathize with the reasons why I was choosing to leave my career to focus on spending time with my kids and re-establish a balance in my life. I was commended for my courage, bravery and desire to put my family and I first and quietly shut the door on a long career where my decisions resulted in me missing out on so much.

To many of the women who sought me out, I was living a fantasy they also had. Women I didn't know began to reach out to me when they heard my story and wanted to find out how I came to the decision to leave and what my plans (and fears) were for the future. What was my turning point? I became overwhelmed with the number of women who, like me, were unhappy with their current lifestyles but felt they could not let go, riddled by many of the same fears that I had. I was more surprised when I realized that many of these women, all extremely talented and intelligent, were like me in that they suffered from a lack of faith and belief in themselves and their skills, could not identify what they really wanted, or where in various positions within their personal lives where they were unable to make a change which, ultimately, caused an imbalance in their lives as well. For some, they wanted more or something different from more time to being able to work from home, to changing their family dynamics or overcoming a fear but did not feel that they knew how to get it or were afraid to go get it.

By sharing my story with others, I began to realize that I was not alone in creating artificial limits on what we, as women, could do. As women, we are amazing! Our primitive limbic responses make us nurturers and attend to the needs of others before ourselves. We constantly make sacrifices for others. For me, sacrificing for others gave me a false sense of being needed and important, stroking my ego when I was tired and frustrated, causing me to believe that what I was doing was right, and that I cared too much to ignore helping others because that was only "the right thing to do." I ignored the many warnings that the life I was leading and the decisions I was making over almost two decades was starting to veer too far away from the path I should be on, to the detriment of my personal health and relationships.

I have always wanted to help and support others. With my new-found time, I knew I wanted to focus on this but was not clear on how I could do it. As I talked with women across a wide range of ages, professional careers and stages of their lives, I was aghast to learn that they shared the same thoughts and feelings that I did. After hearing their stories, the dots started to connect that would become the catalyst to re-fuelling a burning desire that I once had of doing something extraordinary: fulfilling my teenage desire of wanting to write a book.

With all the energy, thoughts and creative visions that encircled me once I made the decision to get off the path I had been travelling on, I needed help to straighten out what seemed like a tangled and foggy road ahead of me with no obvious signs directing me where to go. To help me start over, I put my belief and faith into the person who had planted the seed of change in me many months before. She had had her own battles that she had fought and won, so I sought out her knowledge, experience and support as a safe haven. Because I wanted to ensure I had clarity on the life I was starting to envision, I sought out the assistance of another mentor to help me trudge through the behaviors that were negatively impacting me. I became adept at being able to analyze why I had certain negative habits and paradigms and how these were having a negative impact on my life and bringing me negative experiences. By looking deeper into the source of my paradigms and behaviors I started to identify actions to take to consciously re-build my habits and paradigms, to start being aware of what being happy felt like and then carving out a plan to define and execute my goal of doing something extraordinary. I began to nurture myself into a woman who continues to surprise me on a daily basis

Along this journey of self-discovery and growth I learned a lot about what had led me to where I was in life and why I was not happy. I learned what skills and behaviors I needed to nurture and develop in order to foster my personal growth and happiness. With reflection, I can honestly say I do not regret the choices and paths I had taken to this point in my life. They had introduced me to my friends, my husband and gave me my children and rich learning experiences. These experiences also provided me with skills and lessons that I would be able to benefit from as I strove forward in a new direction. So not all was lost during the years I spent on my off-roading experience. I just wished I had been driving a four-by-four or wearing a helmet. There might have been less damage.

I love looking in the mirror now at who I have become, a stark contrast to the person I used to see in my reflection which was a person I did not recognize and to be honest, did not always like. I have become a woman with a desire to share my story with other women and help them to realize that they are not alone in feeling "stuck" in their lives. Through the sharing of my trials, tribulations and successes I want to be able to help plant a seed in the minds of women around the world. And like the seed that was planted in my mind and left to germinate until I was ready to nurture and grow it, to help other women grow better balance for their lives. A seed that may have been stagnant but was now awakening to a new sense of self, sharing the lessons crucial to me in drawing out the topography of who I wanted to be and who I wanted around me, supporting the awesome brand new me.

Not only did I connect with a desire to help and empower other women to believe in themselves, I wanted to look at the bigger picture and share stories and learning opportunities with young girls in the hopes that they would gain the knowledge to be comfortable with themselves, to break down their barriers and to feel that they can do what they want to do in life. As I know all too well, to not be happy with yourself at a young age sets you up for a long, arduous adult life.

Many of the doubts, fears and barriers I encountered throughout my life stemmed from not learning as a girl how to believe in myself and who I was, doing what I was told versus taking risks and challenging myself. The impact was that I spent a large part of my life feeling awkward and out of place in the very life I was mapping out for myself. The decisions I was making seemed to take me further away from something I could not put my finger on. For many of the "big" decisions I made in my life, I had done so knowing, but never outwardly sharing with anyone, that they did not feel right. I made decisions based on how people saw me, what I was being told would be good for me, what I thought others wanted me to do, what the next logical step would be and what might help me to forget the parts of myself that I was embarrassed about. So many times, deep down I wanted somebody to grab me and tell me to "stop!" What I eventually learned was that how I viewed myself was creating and causing the actions and environments that were making me unhappy in my life. Action = Reaction. What I have since learned is that I had a lot of difficulty being positive about myself because I had dramatically altered my subconscious perception of myself and did not see my self-image as positive.

So this book is also about a journey of self-discovery and how I changed my rules in order to create a new type of success for myself.

It is about me becoming consciously aware of the habits and paradigms that were causing my unhappiness. It was not my environment, my peers, my work or my family situation causing my unhappiness. It was me and how I was thinking and a warped perception of who I was and what I needed to do that was driving my behaviors to be inefficient and ineffective. Steeping back, it is amazing how much clarity can be gained. And that is what I needed. It is about what changes I began to realize were needed in order to pull me onto a path where I could build up myself and make a quantum jump into an empowered woman, confident in her ability to help others. And these were not logical, sequential changes. Some of the actions I took were completely illogical and contradicted lessons that I had always been taught. This book is about my development and transition from being an extra in the movie of my life to me directing and starring in it. It is about me having the desire to use critical reflection and storytelling to share my experiences so that I might potentially help other women become strong in their vision of who they are and then extend that desire and vision to our impressionable young girls.

Everyone deserves the opportunity to learn how to be self-confident. For girls and women, I believe this is even more important as we, as a gender, still face many obstacles and barriers that exist in society and in our own minds. I want to share with women and girls the life lesson that, when you learn how to build up your self-esteem, your barriers can be knocked down. This book was written with the belief and desire that as a strong woman, you can empower both yourself and the mind of a young girl (or girls) in your life, to develop, reconnect and believe in yourselves for who you really are. And that you both can achieve whatever it is you truly want in life.

Our girls need and deserve to be confident with who they are. We need to arm them with the arsenal of emotional intelligence and leadership skills that they will need to make decisions with confidence in any situation they come across in their lives, whether in the schoolyard, classrooms, teams and all the way into the boardroom or shop floor. In order for our girls to develop these skills, they need strong women to look up to as role models. Women who are willing to develop and strengthen themselves and be vulnerable enough to share their stories of success and challenges as learning opportunities. As part of the validation that I needed when I was resigning, I looked at my children and saw how my physical and emotional absence was not providing them with consistent positive reinforcement because I was either absent or too emotionally drained to support them and their needs. They were a reflection of me; frustrated and not happy and I was determined to stop the cycle.

I had always wanted to show my children that you needed to have a hard work ethic in order to do well in life and be successful. That was the belief that I grew up with. Work hard, put in your time and do what you are told. Unfortunately, what I had shown them was that working hard meant being tired and cranky, and absent or late to family activities. I had demonstrated to them that working was perceived to be more important than they were. What a complete backfire! As I studied myself, and through the writing of this book, I wanted to re-direct the focus of what I was teaching my children and show them that it is crucial to believe in whom you are in order to follow the desires and dreams that would make them happy. That to achieve happiness and success, you didn't need to work harder. At the end of the day, who they choose to be and what they choose to do for a living, they needed to be happy with their choices, not relegated to doing something because it had made logical sense to do so, or been what somebody else had wanted for them or they were afraid of taking risks. I am now working on teaching my kids that following your desires and dreams requires work, taking on and defeating the challenges that stand in your way and may take years to complete. At the end of the journey, happiness will walk beside you if self-belief supports you.

I realize that I made many mistakes along the tumultuous path that I originally carved out for myself. My hope is that readers will connect with one or all of my stories. As a woman, to know that you are not alone in situations that may have left you feeling confused, disoriented or disconnected with the life that you are living is important. I truly hope that some will be able to learn from my mistakes in order to avoid the same fate, or that an opportunity or idea will be presented that you can take action on personally or professionally.

The fact that you have made the choice to read this book is an action that shows you want to reflect on your current professional and/or personal state and what has led you to be in the position that you are in, that you want more out of life and want to grow. As this book is a melding of stories for women and girls to be used in conjunction with each other, you are more than likely reading this book because you have a desire to help yourself while being a positive role model for the next generation of women. Celebrate your commitment to this, as there are only positive outcomes that await the improvement of yourself and the enrichment of the life of somebody else.

Storytelling and the sharing of tales to impart knowledge has been a dramatic and powerful learning tool used by an expansive array of cultures for thousands of years. I am a believer in using storytelling and reflection as a method of experiential or transformational learning. To make learning so powerful that it drives down into the subconscious and changes how we think and behave. My stories are meant to share tales of wisdom, battle, raging mental, physical and emotional wars and triumphant wins, while hopefully also providing a little bit of entertainment along the way.

The use of reflection questions throughout the chapters is designed to provide you and the young girl you are mentoring with the opportunity to critically reflect on your thoughts and images, your perceptions and the source of your beliefs and of yourself at a moment in time. The questions are also phrased to assist you in trying to visualize in your mind what it is you want. Reflecting may motivate you to commend yourself for the positive strides you have already made in your life, to analyze where you would like to challenge yourself personally or professionally or, at least, to get you to spend time on yourself and your memories of yesteryears (or yesterday) and bring some balance back into your life.

By reflecting with your young girl, she is learning from your experiences and can become connected to you and your ideas, and you in turn gain the opportunity to see what ideas and beliefs shape her thoughts and behaviors, where and how you can support her and where you can encourage and congratulate her! Sharing one story, one thought, one reflection could cause a ripple effect on your decision making to go after what you want. A ripple effect that could result in your young girl forming an idea or plan to go after what she really wants. How amazing is that?

I caution that neither you nor your special young girl will change overnight. It took years to create the people the two of you are, so to change habits, paradigms and resulting thoughts and behaviors can take time.

As I worked to change myself, my energy and emotional capacity grew and some results were visibly noticeable to others faster than others. Other results took me awhile to grow accustomed to and confident enough in to share. I then started to use the strategies that were helping me to become confident with my children. It took a conscious effort, but I consistently reinforced my positive behavior and recognized theirs. I continue to reflect on what I can do to better grow as an individual and assess what my children need for support. My persistence with my development and ability to influence that of my children paid off as I could soon see their behavior changing. Something as simple as having them write their beliefs down and recite them made them realize that they had control over their emotions and behavior. As you work through this book, be persistent in focusing on the positive behaviors you see in yourself and your young girl. When you have finished with this book, go back and read it together again, answering the reflection questions again. As you both grow in your awareness of yourselves, the wealth of your experiences will grow and your reflective learning will become even more powerful and impactful. Each time you work through a chapter, you will each bring new stories to share, discuss and learn about together.

I do not regret for one moment the stray paths and journeys I have taken in my life. I do not blame anyone for the experiences I had to endure. It was these experiences that brought me to where I was, with two beautiful children, and a trunk full of knowledge and wisdom that I am now just starting to open, rifle through, try on for size and share with others. I could have easily chosen to continue to live my life looking around the corner for the next opportunity with a wish that it would bring me closer to all-round happiness. But as I reflect back, I can see how the path of my life is all connected and my experiences were necessary to bring me to the crux of my decision to forge forward from being the person I was not happy with, and to take the leap of faith necessary to re-discover my passions and dreams and identify what I truly was meant to do with my life.

I do not regret making the quantum leap. My children are a daily reminder that I made the right choice. Loving the person that I see in the mirror is an amazing and uplifting experience. Being able to share my stories to help empower women to empower girls is fulfilling my desire to help others plant strong roots in who we are as women and girls to withstand the storms, droughts and pollution that surround our everyday lives and challenges the core strength of who we are. To intertwine the dreams and stories of women and girls sharing their experiences with each other in a powerful mentoring dynamic extends my dream of helping others into a whole other dimension.

I no longer believe that I was meant to do something great. I know that I was meant to do something extraordinary.

PART I

INSPIRE YOURSELF AND DISCOVER YOUR MENTORING TALENTS

1

Sharing this Book: Recommendations for the Mentor

The mantra of this book is "Empowering Women Empowering Girls." As such, it is focused on providing stories and inspiration to enrich the lives and experiences of three entities: the mentor (the woman, or you), the mentee (the girl you are taking this journey with) and the mentor-mentee dyad.

There are two further sections to this book, each with eight chapters of stories, reflections and lessons that parallel the same themes and knowledge. Learning opportunities I had that provided important lessons for me are included; lessons I sometimes adhered to and lessons that I completely ignored. As I started to write this book, I realized that, in some situations, I had missed the value of their presence at the time and how, because I did not believe in myself, trust in my ability to make the right decision or just did what I was told, I made decisions that were not aligned with what would make me happy.

Let's start with empowering you, the mentor.

Read one chapter from the "For You – The Mentor" section and reflect on the questions throughout the chapter. Assess if you already are in possession of the trait or knowledge of the lesson shared in the chapter in order to empower you or validate your belief in your inner strength. Then sit with your mentee and read the parallel chapter in the "For Her - The Mentee" section together, out loud. Read the chapter to your mentee, or have both of you share in reading out loud. Have fun with it as this is time for the two of you to share and connect.

Answer the reflection questions together to help your mentee to discover or renew her strengths and build a powerful dialogue between the two of you. If desired, write your answers down so that you may return to them at a later time and reflect on them. I recommend keeping a separate journal of your experiences. Move through the book at a pace that is comfortable for you and your mentee.

As this is a journey for you and your mentee you can stop and reflect on one chapter longer than you may do on another. Use your intuition to guide your time. Review your thoughts and potential actions that you wrote down. Start to visualize what it is that both of you are searching for. Draw what you see or would like to see. Share with each other what your dreams and desires look like. If the other person can picture what you are saying, you are providing clarity to your dream and something you can target and go after. As you change your belief in yourselves, write it down. Re-read what you have written to re-affirm the positive feelings and thoughts you have for yourselves and each other. Be grateful for the time you are taking for yourself and your special girl. It is time that cannot be taken away. Like grains of sand falling quickly in the hourglass, time passes, and so do opportunities to go after what each of you want.

By working as part of a mentoring dyad you will be able to stand together and plant the seeds for your ideas and develop roots for your dreams. As you both nurture your dreams, your roots will grow and, if you let them, they can intertwine together and create a foundation of strength exponentially more powerful than a single root system on its own. A strong root system will allow you to stand tall and be proud of whom you are, and keep you erect as your own storms, or the storms of others, wail on you and challenge your strength.

Enjoy the wisdom that you are going to gain from listening to yourself, the wisdom that you can pass onto the powerful young girl you have committed yourself to helping, and the fortuitous journey of self-discovery that both of you are embarking on. Observe the potential development of emotional closeness and provision fostered through the sharing and reflection of stories.

Embrace the time that you have committed to growing yourself, your mentee and your relationship with her. Your memories will become a reflection of this time and the actions that you took to go after your dreams.

2

Storytelling, Reflecting and Mentoring as Learning Tools

The basis of this book uses storytelling, reflection and mentoring to provide a breadth of learning formats that touch on many of the ways that adults, teens and children can learn, each with their different levels of conception and understanding. The more ways information can be provided increases its capability of being cognitively digested at the conscious level, and increases its ability to migrate into the subconscious where it can impact habits and behaviors by providing an emotional connection to a learning opportunity.

I use storytelling and reflection throughout this book in order to provide you and your mentee with opportunities to connect or relate to my experiences and compare or contrast it to your own experiences. Perhaps I did something you can implement into your own life. Through the mentoring experience that this book provides, you take your turn using storytelling and personal reflection to guide discussions with your mentee to learn from you, and you will in turn learn from her stories and reflections. These three concepts of storytelling, reflection and mentoring are continuously woven together throughout this book in a cyclical manner to scaffold your learning, help guide and build the foundation for the belief and actions you may need to pursue your dreams, identify and support your mentee in her goals, and provide a format for you and your mentee to connect emotionally to each other and build a relationship from intertwined connections and experiences.

When I returned to school as an adult to complete my Bachelor of Education in Adult Education, I began to understand the concept of using storytelling as a tool for learning. This was a vastly different learning experience from the instructor-led lectures or hands-on laboratory formats I experienced during my undergraduate science degree. I had always enjoyed listening to the stories of others in conversations but I had not to that point really experienced learning from storytelling in an academic setting. I was biased from my only other university experience and assumed that how I was taught, and how I learned years earlier, would be the same.

Not so. What I realized after a few weeks in my first course was that if I quizzed myself I could remember the material we were being taught and make connections between the lessons. I learned all this without my professor standing at the front of the classroom and lecturing the class. Like awe-inspiring architecture, the design and delivery of the course curricula was designed in a manner that required willing participation by the entire class in storytelling. A safe learning environment was created for a group of strangers to be comfortable enough to open up and share their stories with one another. I perceived that I had become part of a powerful learning community that I felt lasted for the entire duration of my degree.

We see examples of storytelling as a method of teaching and learning throughout our media, in training courses or even with friends as we catch up over cup of coffee or glass of wine. Television shows exemplify this method through the development and use of a main character, typically a veteran in their respective field within the context of the show, who imparts knowledge to subordinates and peers through the sharing of stories of experience and adapted knowledge of a finite situation--information too finite to be taught in a textbook and requiring real-life experiences to fully understand and make an emotional connection to so that it can be transformational. Often these television stories are based on real-life facts and truths and, even as a viewer, you end up sharing in the learning experience with the fictional characters, gaining new knowledge of something you didn't know 30 seconds earlier. How many times have you caught yourself sharing this television knowledge to others via a casual "Hey, I learned on this show that..."and so the storytelling carries forth to its next group of engaged learners.

Many of the training courses I have been on throughout my professional career included elements of storytelling where participants were asked, willingly and sometimes unwillingly, to share their experiences to provide a real-life scenario or connection to the concept being taught. Not only does storytelling take the focus of the group off the trainer or facilitator as a means of a break in attention, but it uses the concept that experiences are more common at the individual level than perceived, and that everyone has a different method for reacting or responding to a common experience. Storytelling can provide unknown learning opportunities in passing on tidbits of information you can then adapt into your personal or professional life to make it better.

Reflection is a popular tool used in training courses, although it is not typically referred to as such. In my experience, people can become uncomfortable reflecting, especially if it is forced. However, anytime you have to review a question and write an answer down as part of a training exercise, you are using reflection to answer the question. You are making a connection between your experience and the content or purpose of your training course. You might have been asked to compare the similarities and differences between case studies to understand and apply the training content, and then come up with an outcome. That is using reflection to learn from the past to amplify present learning and future application.

At a high level, during reflection you learn from the experience. Reflection can provide clarity and insight into your behavior or how you see yourself in a given situation so that you identify the learning opportunity and use it to change your outcome the next time you are in the same or similar situation. Reflection can then be taken to a deeper level to question and understand your ingrained habits and paradigms that caused you to behave or react a certain way to a particular situation.

Through a deep reflective process, I began to dissect and analyze how and what caused me to form specific habits and paradigms. I used reflection to understand the impact of my behavior on my social and personal environments, how it played out in relationships and in actions that I completed.

By reflecting on my career progression, I was able to identify that I had changed roles and career direction many times because I was looking for something that would provide the personal fulfillment that I was yearning for. I dug down and analyzed how my lack of belief in myself, and the conviction that you need to work hard to be successful, were causing me to make decisions that were actually directing me away from an ultimately fulfilling career that aligned with the dreams I had so many years ago. I unknowingly at the time made some strides towards what I was passionate about but I didn't realize it until I had time to reflect on my career as a whole. I had created biased values and ideas as to who I could be. I questioned the "how's" and "why's" behind my actions, thoughts and behaviors and connected them to how they impacted myself, others and the various environments I was in. With the help of my own mentors, I was able to identify what was keeping me rooted where I was personally and professionally, and what I needed to do to make changes.

Mentoring already exists formally or informally in learning environments such as apprenticeship programs, schools, outreach organizations and workplaces. The outcome of mentoring is growth and personal development through the transfer of knowledge, skill and behavior from the mentor to the mentee, with growth occurring in the mentor, mentee and the mentoring relationship. As a mentor, you have the ability to increase your awareness and confidence in your own leadership skills and capabilities. By relying on the depth of wisdom acquired from your own personal experiences and the underlying skills you use on a daily basis (such as leadership, communication, compassion, your desire to help foster the growth and development of someone else), these skills and behaviors can provide the supportive environment needed in a mentoring relationship.

For the mentee, mentoring has been proven to positively impact academic, emotional and social achievements, confidence and leadership capabilities and minimize negative behaviors. The key ingredients for a fruitful relationship, however, are your desire to be a mentor, the fostering of good communication between the two of you and an understanding of what it is that each of you wants to get out of the relationship.

Mentors take the leadership role within the mentor-mentee relationship (the "dyad") and must learn how to flex their presence based on the needs of the mentee. Mentors, however, are not there to fix the mentee's problems. Mentees must learn how to problem-solve and take action themselves, which a mentor can then support by providing suggestions and nurturing the mentee through her actions. Avoid taking the learning opportunity away from her as girls need to learn, practice and refine these skills! Girls also need to learn that it is okay to make mistakes, as they are full of life lessons. Making mistakes can result in a mentee becoming more confident in making decisions and realizing when she needs to ask for help. As a mentor, be there to cushion her fall, a cheerleader to get her back into the game and her biggest fan when she succeeds.

While mentoring is a two-way relationship, it impacts the growth of three entities: the mentor, the mentee and the dyad. The strength of the relationship comes from the dyad as it is the blending and growth of the two people in the relationship that is exponentially more than just two people communicating with each other. It is the increasing of the knowledge, power, confidence and impact of three forces, not one.

As a mentor, you have the opportunity to increase the effectiveness your communication styles (listening, questioning and clearly verbalizing thoughts), to increase your confidence in your own skills and knowledge, to understand how others learn (which may be different than how you learn yourself) and to learn from the information that is shared with you by the mentee. It could be learning the latest in pop culture, for example, or how the mentee is feeling about specific social issues of the day. The learning potential to the mentor is limitless and can be truly amazing because your mentee is opening up, talking and sharing her thoughts with you which, if you were not in this relationship, you might never have experienced.

In order to set the mentor-mentee relationship up for success, the goal or outcome of the relationship needs to be established at the beginning. The mentee needs to understand why the mentor wants to help them and what role they are to play. The mentee needs to be aware of what is expected of them; they need to know that they will have to share their ideas and that the mentor will be there to listen and not judge, to hear opinions but not form an opinion of their own.

The mentor needs to understand how the mentee wants to communicate, and if the mentee wants time to answer the reflection questions themselves then share with the mentor--or work on them together. The mentor needs to understand that they might not be able to answer all the questions that the mentee poses and that that is okay. Mentors are not meant to have all the answers, but they are meant to help the mentee discover what the questions are.

As a mentor, think about how you would like to be mentored. Maybe you once had that privilege, or currently have a mentor via a friend or workmate. By reflecting on how you would like to be mentored, you have a good starting point or frame of reference for embarking on your mentoring journey. And what a journey it will be!

Be prepared for either you or your mentee to be initially hesitant with reflecting and sharing thoughts, let alone dreams and desires. Remember, any information that is shared is more than you previously knew. Small steps can lead to quantum leaps and bounds. Figure out how your dyad will work; it will be unique to the two of you. Be aware that your relationship will change over time as you become more confident in your role as the mentor and intuitively know what your mentee's needs are as your mentee starts to build her confidence and the ability to reflect and think about what she wants.

Start with reflecting on why you want to be inspired and how you want to help your mentee, then use your storytelling to lead your mentee through her own reflections. Take your first steps on your journey to empower you, empower her, and empower each other.

Get inspired and go after what you both really want.

3

The Beginning: Tearing Down

"I want to play hockey."

I made the statement as a young girl to a group of women standing around an arena lobby in-between hockey games for one of my brothers. A little voice interrupting the adult conversation going on around me. I don't know what gave me the courage to speak up at that moment, but I did. While some of the women smiled at me and others ignored me, I did hear one comment spoken very nicely but in a way to correct my course of thinking. .

"That is interesting! Good for you but I'm sorry honey, girls don't play hockey. They play ringette."

Standing in that arena for what was just one of many hockey games in my lifetime, I made the decision that I, too, wanted to play hockey. I had heard at school that there was a small girls' hockey program just starting up in my hometown and for some reason, even being the introvert that I was, I wanted to get in on the action. That dream, though, was stopped dead in its tracks in that one moment. And I gave up.

I didn't want to play ringette. Even with its similarity to hockey, I had absolutely no interest in playing. Although I dreaded being dragged around to arenas for my brothers' games, I secretly liked hockey and wanted to learn how to play. I had taken skating lessons and was good, at least in my books. I had no interest in figure skating (I was not the graceful type) and felt that hockey better suited me. It may have been because with an older and younger brother and lots of boys in the neighbourhood, I would join in on the friendly road hockey games in front of my house. At the time, nobody ever wanted to be goalie so, I got stuck in net a lot. In hindsight, I did not mind this. From informal playing on the road, I wanted to transition to playing on the ice. Making the decision to play hockey was easy. It was the asking part that was difficult as I feared the response that I would get. And in the end, I got just the response I feared.

I grew up in a time when society had a firm belief in the roles of boys and girls and propagated certain gender stigmas. At the time, I had heard that there was a small girls' hockey organization in my hometown that was trying to grow the sport for girls and I wanted to get involved.

I remember thinking that because my brothers wanted to play hockey, they got to play hockey and that just because I was a girl it was not mainstream to let me play hockey. I didn't understand why it was so unfair. Being struck down so quickly with my dream to play hockey really hit a nerve with me. It is amazing how one situation can bother you for a lifetime.

Being told that girls did not play hockey had an impact not only on a dream I had, but also on my self-belief. I was a quiet kid so to voice my opinion on something I already knew would not be met with warmth and support was a big deal to me. With one response, my dream was shattered and how I felt about myself was changed.

It is amazing that, even now, decades later, I can envision that moment when I shared my dream. I can even remember the arena I was in. What I recognize now is that I have many situations when I did stand up for myself and do what I wanted to do, and did it emphatically because I was a girl. My husband would refer to me as "Millennium Woman" when I balked at simple, courteous actions on his part (e.g., hold the door open for me), expressing that "I can hold my own door open" or carry a 50 pound landscaping rock by myself. In any situation where I stood up for my beliefs and myself, I felt empowered and sure of myself. But in those situations where I did not stand up for my beliefs, it created turmoil within me over time. It impacted how I saw myself and, in some cases, I was no longer able to recognize the person I had become. Unfortunately, any moments of being self-confident as a child were few, overridden by negative thoughts and beliefs about myself, about what I could and could not do, and who I was--and was not.

The destruction of belief in yourself can be swift or it can chip away at you over time. For me, this blemish in my confidence resulted in a slow drip of feelings of self-worth or importance right out of my soul. As a child, I felt like I had nobody to talk to about how I was feeling, or to help me understand what I was feeling. As a result, I grew up sad, confused, not confident or sure of different aspects of who I was and someone who looked for guidance but was afraid to ask for help. Parents and teachers were not equipped then with the knowledge they have now. I feel that in society today we are more aware now as women, parents, educators and mentors of how a lack of confidence and belief in oneself, especially in impressionable young girls, can impact emotional, spiritual and mental growth.

The dreams and desires I had growing up were only re-fuelled when a support system I desperately was in need of appeared in my adult life. Once I started to regain a belief in myself, based on the belief that others had in me, I again developed the courage I had as that little girl letting that group of women know that I wanted to play hockey. And this time, I was not taking "no" for an answer. It took the support and encouragement of others for me to take a good look at myself and permanently alter the direction I had been going in. Misdirection caused by decisions based on fear or lack of belief in my knowledge and skills had to be overcome. With a newfound desire to use my experience to help others, I trekked out a new path for myself in the direction I wanted it to go.

I want to take you with me on the journey.

Think of one experience in your life that has broken down your belief in yourself. Why did that one experience come to mind? Who was the experience with? What was the situation and what emotions did you feel were attacked? As a mentor, why have you decided now to re-build belief in yourself? What has happened in your life to make you want to become a stronger woman than what you are now?

PART II

For You - The Mentor

4

Desires and Dreams

Remember your first love as a little girl? The giddiness that would bubble up from the pit of your stomach then exit as a high-pitched giggle? Hiding your head behind the nearest object or into the crook of your shoulder if that "special someone" happened to glance your way? Your whole world and biggest wish revolved around the potential glance or perhaps few words spoken to you by the one you focused your heart's desire on. Not knowing how, why or what made this person special was not even part of your thought process. Who cared? Certainly not you! None of this information mattered as you simply had this desire for someone and that was all that you needed to know.

Now, fast-forward a few years.

School, life, career and family--maybe you have all of these. Or maybe you have only some of these. But if you are reading this book it is with the assumption that you are reading it along with a young girl you care deeply for. It may be your daughter. It may be somebody else's daughter. It may be a student. It may be somebody not at all related to you but who you know needs a supportive mentor in her life right now. The definition of the relationship between you and this special young girl is of no importance. What is important is that you have a desire to want to role model the behaviors to this girl that will set her up with the knowledge, skills and belief in herself to face the challenges and roadblocks that will come her way. You want to provide the nurturing support of someone who is aware of the dangers, pitfalls and negative persuasion that lurk around every corner, in every schoolyard and in every workplace. You want to impart the power of knowledge and self-belief to yourself and to somebody else who needs it.

At this point in your life, what is it that you desire? What were your dreams as a little girl or teenager? Is there anything that you really want? Perhaps it is a want that you have hidden in the depths of your subconscious that you may be embarrassed about and have not shared with anybody. Or a want that you talk about on a day-to-day basis with friends as in "maybe next year when I find the time I will…," but you never seem to find that time or make it a priority. And the story is getting old, but you are not able to convert the want from fantasy to one of action. When you think about that thing, that person, that want and you still do not go after it, how does that make you feel?

What is your first memory of going after something you had a burning desire to have or do? When was the last time you acted on a burning desire with no fear of consequence? What do you desire right now?

Can you think of examples for one or all of these questions? If you can, close your eyes and think about how you felt when you first got that thought in your head to desire something. Have you previously attained what you desired? If so, how did you feel when you achieved it? If you have not attained the object of your desire, why is that?

If you were not able to think of examples for any of the questions, can you identify why? What is stopping you from believing in something so much that you want it more than anything else? Who is stopping you?

In order to answer these questions, you need to get honest with yourself. Completely raw with your emotions. The great thing about your dreams and desires is that they have no boundaries, biases or prejudices. They are irrelevant of age, race, culture, orientation or perceived intellectual capacity. They cannot be willed or forced. They are natural and spontaneous and, like a genetic blueprint, are completely unique to you.

There is absolutely nothing wrong with having a burning desire to go after something. It is not selfish. It is not ignorant. Desire is a feeling created by you, for you, to lift you up into the throes of the emotions that will drive you to act and do things beyond your current capabilities in order to achieve something larger than what you currently have. Barring any safety or compliance aspects related to what you desire, there is inexhaustible learning that you will experience if you seek the path that leads to what you desire. People, knowledge and skills will be presented to you along your journey, completely enriching the experience of your desire without you even realizing it.

Focus on the object of your desire. It may be something that you want for yourself, or for somebody else. Perhaps you have a desire to help the girl that you are reading this book with. It may be a new car, a promotion, meeting a business goal, challenging a fear or wanting to try something you have always wanted to do. It may be something you wanted to do a lifetime ago that you thought was no longer possible. What is this desire? If you haven't done so already, write it down.

Something I wanted and desired to do when I was in my teens was to write a book. I wanted to write teenage romance novels in order to infuse the fantasy of romance into what was a pretty lackluster love life up to that point in my young life. I had even started brainstorming plotlines, characters and settings. In any scenario I thought up, my main character was named Samantha (I was obsessed with that name as a teen). The plotline would always revolve around forbidden love, being with the popular boy who made all the girls swoon and was the "right choice" but secretly desiring the reclusive, husky boy who made a point to not follow the status quo. Sigh. Unfortunately, these characters and stories did not come to life for more than a few pages before I closed the proverbial book on my writing career which was something I kept hidden from all but a few, and something that, although I had a desire to do it, was embarrassed about. I let my feelings of embarrassment and a feeling I was too inexperienced to write romance novels to outweigh my desire to write and, once I graduated from high school, I put my pen and paper away for a long time.

Around my 40th birthday, I wrestled up the courage to get completely raw and honest with myself, just as I am asking you to do. I asked myself the same questions I asked you. What did I desire right now? What was my dream? What was holding me back? I had not spent time asking myself those questions in a really long while, probably because I was afraid the truth or knew that I would be just lying to myself. I had made a career out of working hard and working too much to spend time thinking about what I really wanted as I focused instead on what others wanted and needed.

The seed of my ancient desire to write a book may have been buried deep but the embers were still burning. This time, it was not a teenage romance I desired to write (romance, mystery men and exotic heroes had all played out in my life).This time, I wanted to write a book for women and girls based on my experiences growing up as a teen and throughout adulthood. I wanted to write a book that would empower women and girls of all ages to identify and go after what it was that they truly desired. To break through or leap over the barriers they felt were trapping them and find the motivation and drive to attain even more. I want females to believe that they can challenge themselves and the box they have drawn around themselves and their ideas, and break it all down to become stronger and wiser. My desire is to help other women learn that their desires, when completely honest and when acted upon, have the opportunity to provide them with a self-belief system that can result in further challenges and immeasurable rewards. More importantly, I want to provide women and girls with the knowledge and empowerment that they can do whatever they put their mind to. The learning potential of going after what you desire and dream for is infinite!

You have the capacity and capabilities to go after exactly what you want. Because if you really couldn't do something, the idea would never have been presented to you. It is only the limitations you put on yourself that is your barrier. In order to go after what you want, you need to be able to visualize it as already existing and already yours. It's your dream after all. It now becomes your choice whether you move forward and get what you want, or stay in your current position. It is scary, it is uncomfortable, and it may require you to be unconventional in your thoughts and behaviors to go get what you want.

I experienced all of these emotions and behaviors as I drove forward writing this book and achieving my dream. But as you start to move towards what you want, people, things, ideas, links and connections will effortlessly begin to appear for you. Can you imagine yourself with skills and knowledge you would never have challenged yourself with before? Can you feel the excitement and energy that you would create within yourself as you strove towards your goal? Can you imagine yourself as you, only better?

What is your story that you will be able to look back at and write someday? Don't let another day go by where you talk about the "what ifs" and "it would be great if I...". Stop adding ideas to your "should 'a, would 'a, could 'a" pile and start making an "I did" pile.

Start today with being honest with yourself and asking one simple question: what is it that I desire? What is my dream?

5

Believing in Yourself

I am Catholic (albeit not a practicing one). I was born into a Catholic family and went to Catholic schools. Like many religions, I believe in a God I was taught stories about but have never actually seen. My belief or faith in God is synonymous with the definition that I trust something exists that I cannot see. I just know that God exists, because my belief tells me it is right.

As a child, you are at the mercy of learning from the environment that surrounds you as you take in information without any ability to filter it. This information is what forms the foundation of your likes and dislikes as well as your beliefs or faith. As a child you naturally believed what you were told. That is how you made the connections between things and believed: the sky is blue, the grass is green, the sun is yellow and things like a God exist. Your mind as a child has no filter that would cause you to modify your belief system.

We exhibit belief on a daily basis without giving a second thought to it. Belief that a friend will support you when you are in a crisis, belief that your spouse will remember your birthday, belief in yourself that you will meet a deadline or keep a promise. Belief is a confidence you exude when you trust in something or someone. You have it or you don't. When you have it, it can be a powerful ally in your ability to trust, but when you don't have it, there is scepticism. If it has been lost or wounded, regaining it can be a long, arduous road that you need to continuously work at.

Over the years I had lost belief in myself. I had lost faith and confidence in my ability to handle all that life threw my way and to respond with confidence and ease. Like many women, I had created a vision of being able to do it all without the help of any superpowers. Believe me, if there was a store or online retailer selling superpowers, I'd be standing in line to order a triple-triple of belief, decisiveness and patience (along with a really stylish pair of shoes!).

My lack of belief ran parallel to my lack of confidence. If I was unable to believe I could attain whatever it was I desired at the time, my self-confidence was in a drought-like state and I did not have confidence in my skills or abilities or who I was as a person. To go back to Chapter 4, another one of my desires as a teen was to become a doctor. Specifically, I wanted to be a psychiatrist. I enjoyed, and still enjoy, listening to people's problems and had the desire to help others make sense of what they were thinking and feeling.

I graduated from high school armed with high academic standings in science and math prerequisites, as well as English, and entered university full of energy with a vision of it being the first year of many on the road to medical school. But by the time midterm exams were over in my first semester of my first year, I had lost confidence in my intelligence and any future of being a doctor.

Like many first-time university students, I had assumed that my study habits in high school would fluidly transition into being able to meet the learning expectations at the university level. I was completely wrong. I quickly learned that memory and recall would not cut it in a world where application, critical analysis and connections between theories were expected. I could not graze over my notes and textbooks thinking that all the content would be filtered into my brain. And I need to be honest, I was blind to the reality that nights out at the local establishments every week would impact my academic focus. At the end of my first semester, I received grades of A, B, C, D and F. I was confused and dumbfounded as to how I could go from being such a high achiever to less than average in just a few months. I became that statistic--the urban legend. One of those students who succeeds in high school only to not see that success translated into post-secondary studies. One of those students who, when presented with the freedom that comes with living away from home for the first time, takes advantage of it. I had just assumed that my intellect plus my new freedom would be the best of friends and find a way to work together. In my overwhelmed state, I made the decision that if one semester was this bad there was no way I wanted to have this feeling throughout the remainder of my undergraduate program and then years of medical school. So after my first semester, I gave up on myself, my dream of being a doctor, and the belief I had what it took to be what I desired. I shared my feelings of despair with a few people, but nobody I knew was doing as poorly as me so I figured I was alone. I did not seek help. Instead, I battled alone.

I struggled for the remainder of my undergraduate career, uncomfortable with what I was doing and not able to rebound from my first semester. I created a self-belief that, if I was no longer driven to go to medical school, then my grades were irrelevant. Whether I finished my degree with a 4.0 or 2.0 GPA, it did not matter. I would still attend the same graduation ceremony and receive the same piece of paper as everybody else in my graduating class. I didn't even care about the prospect of attending graduate school. I just wanted to be finished with my undergraduate years and get to work, as my belief in my ability to work hard at a job was still alive. I did not see my academic life like a job. I perceived academics and working to be independent silos and, at the time, was not able to see that the skills for one could be connected to the other. I worked hard to finish my degree but I was not motivated to do the best I could. As I reflect back, I can see how a cycle of depression manifested itself throughout my university career, no doubt debilitating my ability to believe in myself, be confident in my skills and think of a way to crawl out of the hole I was digging myself into.

Have you ever given up on something you dreamed of? What was it? Why did you give up on it? Reflecting back on why you gave up, what could you learn about yourself and how you perceived your situation at the time?

As a teen, I spent the summers with my grandmother working on farms.

It was during that time that I honed my strong work ethic. I had grown up watching my parents work hard for what we had, so that behavior was engrained in me from an early age.

I was a city girl not afraid to get her hands dirty and no job was beneath me to do. I would drive for results and not quit until the work was done. The hours I spent working for other farmers during the day was hard (I de-tasselled corn), and when the day was over, I would return back to my grandmother's house and help her weed her gardens and fields. I can remember grumbling at times about the amount of work that had to be done but I still did it. Even if I didn't want to be working in the fields I relied on my personal desire to do quality work to keep me motivated and focused on getting the job done and done well. I remember being upset when a farmer I was working for critiqued my work and I spent the rest of the day upset that someone had found an error in my work. Although as I reflected back on that moment years later, it really was not a bad critique and the farmer was trying to be helpful and just wanted to make me aware of the situation as it was not typical of my work. I went back to the fields for the rest of the day determined to prove that one incident was not in-dicative of the overall quality of my work. I became confident in my capa-bilities to work hard and produce good results. I remember driving around the countryside looking at other farmers' fields and seeing the amount of weeds in them, feeling proud that my grandmother's fields were the clean-est in the area. The reciprocation of thanks by helping others and being persistent to make sure a job was done well played a role in establishing my work ethic and taught me to be proud of my results.

After graduating from university, I went immediately into a career in a lab testing products. Through the application of my strong work ethic, I quickly became comfortable with the techniques and processes within the lab and my workplace. I found that I enjoyed being able to make the connections between what I had learned in university and the practical ap-plications of what I was doing on a day-to-day basis. I started to become thirsty for more knowledge and skill development that I satiated by earning promotions and changing companies in horizontal, lateral and downward movements in order to continually challenge and feed my desire to learn and find a career that really connected with me and left me feeling fulfilled.

What I discovered early in my professional career was that I had an unconscious desire to frequently change roles. I typically changed jobs, including companies, every two years. I tired of roles quickly even though I knew I still had immense learning capacity left within the role. This continual change in careers did not bother me, it motivated me, as I used the belief in my strong work ethic to drive me to take on new challenges and roles I was confident I could complete, and well. I felt like I was searching for something but didn't know what it was.

I spent my career as a consultant and in industries that I enjoyed, with people that I became friends with. As I grew professionally and started leading people and teams, I could reflect and identify that it was the moments when I was being sought out for assistance, coaching or mentoring, writing or training when I felt most valuable. Using my knowledge and experience to solve problems and to help others pleased me. I began to once again identify that I had a desire to help others solve problems. Only the problems I frequently helped to solve were technical, not personal which is what I had a fondness for and connection to and which drew me to positions where I was able to lead and help others in their own development.

About midway through my career, an advertisement in the local newspaper caught my attention. The ad was to complete a Bachelor of Education in Adult Education degree. Having previously attended university for a science degree, I cannot recall why it caught my attention but I was curious about the program. I checked it out online. I can remember reflective thoughts about wanting to help others playing through my mind. At that point in my career, I was leading a team and not feeling that I was supporting them as effectively as I could. I wanted to do more and better support their needs. I started to focus on what I wanted to get out of going back to school. When I did that, the old desire to help others was rekindled. What I realized was that I wanted to develop my skills to better understand how my adult teams learned so that I could be a better leader for them by increasing the effectiveness of my communications through gaining knowledge about adult learning preferences.

Earning a second degree was never in my plans after graduating with my science degree as my lack of faith in my academic abilities haunted me. Even after applying, I figured I would not be accepted into the program as my GPA met the lower end of the acceptance criteria but I told myself that it would not be high enough. Within a few months of applying, however, I was surprised to see the large envelope in my mailbox from the university, congratulating me on my acceptance and the journey that I was about to take.

On the night of my first class, I remember walking into the classroom scared, overwhelmed and lacking in the belief that I could manage going to school and work full-time. My fear of performing poorly again was at the forefront of my mind and I did not want a repeat (emotionally or academically) of my previous time spent in university. Why is it that, even as adults, situations can pull us back into a past dimension and all those emotions become fresh and real again? I find it amazing how a situation, person or feeling can bring back to my emotional surface feelings that are decades old. I didn't like feeling inept a decade ago and now, without any sense of control over my own emotions, I immediately felt that I was not good enough all over again.

It took only two weeks for me to shed my feelings of insecurity. What I felt going to class for my adult education degree was the exact opposite of what I had felt when attending school for my science degree. Fear was replaced with strength. Doubt was replaced with confidence. My lack of belief in my academic and emotional capabilities disappeared as I was excited to be learning and engaging with my classmates. And my academic results paralleled my excitement. It was during this time that I discovered the power of personal reflection on learning, and that I learned well through the storytelling and experiences shared by my classmates.

The time that it took to finish my Bachelor of Education in Adult

Education degree flew by. Earning that piece of paper meant so much more the second time around because I had ignored my barriers of fear and self-doubt and accomplished more than I even intended. I learned so much about myself at that time, including new interests in adult education and instructional design, that I would be comfortable opening up to my classmates and sharing my experiences with them, now confident I had knowledge that could be shared and seen as value-added to somebody else. It was during this time in my life that my faith in what I knew was restored. I grew to be excited with my knowledge and my ability to teach adults using my problem-solving skills to assess and identify solutions, and deal with learning scenarios instead of technical scenarios. I started to have faith that I was meant to do something with this degree that I could not quite visualize at that time. I started to feel that what I was doing had a purpose and I felt alive.

We should all feel alive in our careers and in our daily lives. Following our desires and going after what we want is empowering and feels amazing! But there are so many obstacles that can be perceived as being in the way of obtaining our desires. Money, education, family, personal feelings about yourself...sound familiar? What are your obstacles? How many of them are ones that you perceive to be an obstacle because you have put it there? What are your fears? When do you feel most alive?

However, as quickly as my faith grew and gave me feelings of empowerment that I could do great things for adult learners, it diminished just as fast. Once out of the routine and support of the classroom, and not being able to apply my new knowledge as frequently as I desired in my everyday work, I slipped back into the routine and once again, was not happy with myself.

For years, I built my career around roles and positions I thought I wanted because it aligned with my science background and was the next obvious choice from a succession planning perspective, and meeting what I thought would provide me with the monetary ability to achieve the work-life balance I sought and the right title to get me to where I thought I wanted to be. Each of these career progressions were met with initial highs and engagement, only to result in frustration and feelings of hopelessness, and a renewal of my lack of faith in myself within a few years.

I constantly felt the pressure as a woman to do it all. I admit I relished being the breadwinner, but was constantly hard on myself for not balancing work, family and kids' activities. In speaking with many of my female friends, those with and without children, they all had one thing in common: the ball that is most commonly dropped is the one that has to do with themselves. Why is it that women seem to give up their own wants and needs in order to help and support others? We as women recognize the blatant fact that we are not taking care of ourselves as best as we can. Together, we need to make further strides in changing that mindset and behavior as heart disease, cancer, mental health and a flurry of other diseases will have no problem taking care of us if we do not find the time to take care of ourselves.

What had become a belief in my strong work ethic had resulted in me identifying who I was as a person through work and this, in fact, become my crutch. Over the years, I somehow began to disconnect myself as a person, mother, wife or friend from what I did as a job and began to identify myself as my job.

I was not the person I thought I would be at 40 when I envisioned the future in my 20s. I was in the role I thought I wanted, with the "right" title, but it was not wholly fulfilling. There were aspects of my job that I loved (e.g., coaching/mentoring a wonderful team; the instructional design of training programs, helping others to learn) but I constantly beat myself up over spending too much time at work and not enough time with my family, and pretty much no time with myself. Lack of sleep trying to do it all turned me into a skeleton of my former self and quite an unpleasant person. I was not happy and, to be honest, I was not even able to define what it was that would make me happy or describe what that feeling could even feel like. I have a servant/leadership philosophy but had taken that philosophy too literally and forgotten that I needed to take care of myself in order to best serve others.

I knew deep down what I needed to do. It was not rocket science but it felt like an enormous undertaking. The summit seemed so far away and I did not feel as though I had all the right equipment, knowledge and skills to start making the climb. Being honest with myself, more than I ever had been in my life, I started to write down what was making me so unhappy, and what I truly desired to do with my life. Once finished, I then had to start re-building the faith and belief in myself that I would be okay. This was difficult as what would be my proof that it even really existed?

I started to continuously tell myself what I needed to be happy and that I needed to find a new path in life that aligned with what I truly desired to do. That all this was possible if I just let go. Let go of the stranger I saw looking back at me in the mirror. Let go of the fear that I would not be successful again. Let go of the belief that my job defined who I was. Let go of ignoring what I needed or not wanting to burden somebody else by asking for help. Let go of the idea I was not confident and did not have faith in my own skills and abilities to do something completely new, and on my own. Let go of worrying about what others would think of me. As I made my climb, I would fall back on my old habit of worrying about what if, when I let go, I just fell, having not properly anchored myself during my climb. What would happen? How could I survive?

All I needed was a little faith in myself. And when I got it, I believed that it was there even though I couldn't see it. When I reached the summit, I let go. And guess what? I didn't fall. I soared. And that became my proof.

What are you hanging onto that is preventing you from having faith in your ability to do something you always desired to do? What would it take for you to let go? What old beliefs about yourself and your habits are preventing you from going after your dream?

What would it take for you to change those thoughts about yourself and your behaviors and have a little faith in yourself?

6

Sticking With it – You CAN Do it!

I was persistent in my quest to find out what I was to do in life. Believe me, with all the different jobs I have had, I have a lot of experience about what I like to do and not do.

I was even persistent in my quest to find what was going to make me happy. I took on the greatest challenge of my life and became a mother but being honest with myself at the time, I was rather convincing in identifying that I was definitely not a stay at home type and had absolute knowledge and belief that I wanted instead to be a working mother. What I did not realize when heading back into the workforce as a working mother was that my drive for a career and my strong work ethic would cause an enormous imbalance in my life that I could never have predicted or imagined.

In 2015 I took my persistence to a whole other level in order to find the career and work-life balance that would make me happy. I initiated an aggressive search to be true to myself and hold nothing back.

After starting my career straight out of university and spending more than two years in the role, I was itching for change and made the first of many career leaps. My career leaps and job changes were pretty frequent. During that time I earned many promotions and climbed corporate ladders. I leaped across industries and specialized fields. I dabbled as a consultant in an industry completely outside what I had come from by using transferable knowledge and skills. I even switched companies for a role that was a considerable demotion in order to have a job in the same city that I lived in.

Early in my career during succession planning discussions with my people leaders I tended to have a short vision when it came to identifying "what I wanted to be when I grew up". For many years I would be asked to plan out my career for the next two, five and 10 years. I always had difficulty planning for 10 years as it seemed like a far-off destination and I was really focused on the "now." "I don't know" was the popular response I had to the question "a manager?" I would propose for the 10-year plan because more often than not, I could not get away with not providing an answer.

I was so naïve about levels and hierarchy at the start of my career. So for the first few years I simply wanted to grow in my technical knowledge and skills and have some title changes to validate my development. I had the philosophy that the business landscape was constantly changing and global growth would provide new opportunities that did not currently exist. I did not want to limit the scope of my career progression to structures and positions existing in current business models. I also did not want to be passed over for a job because I didn't have the "right title" in my succession plan. So instead of identifying the job title I wanted in the future, I started listing characteristics and definitions of what I was looking for in a job: to lead a diverse team, to have the ability to apply technical knowledge to problem solving, to apply adult learning principles, etc. I can now admit I didn't look out further than two years in my career succession planning because I really didn't know what I wanted to do or who I wanted to be. Even as I was getting further into my 30s, I would tell my bosses that I didn't know what I wanted to be when I grew up. It was a little humorous and hid the fact that I was flustered I could not define what job it was that I wanted that would make me feel fulfilled. What I started to realize after completing my Bachelor of Education in Adult Education degree was that adult learning had always had a place in all of the jobs I had previously held and that it was starting to become a growing fixture in my career. I finally identified that I wanted to be more connected to educating others and helping others to learn.

Did you have a dream job as a kid and were able to attain it? If so, what steps did you take to stay on that path? Where did you find that you needed to be persistent (e.g., studies, believing in yourself, learning how to network)? And if you have not yet attained your childhood dream job, why? Why were you not able to "stick with it?"

I was told many times throughout high school, university and in my business career that I would be a good teacher. At one point in my career, a student I interacted with from time to time was finishing her work placement and returning to school. Before she left she said to me that she would love to have "Professor Joworski" teaching one of her classes. I laughed at the time and thanked her for the compliment. It was ironic, though, because I was already starting to ponder returning to school to acquire a graduate degree in a field related to education, as lecturing at the post-secondary level part-time was intriguing to me. I had contemplated being a teacher at one point during high school, but quickly wrote it off as a profession because my mother was a teacher and so were many of my family members, and I figured there were enough teachers in the family. I smile now as I have to be honest and admit that, with all the persistence I used to stay away from the same career that a lot of my family was in, I was always integrating teaching and learning into my careers anyway and now am aligning more and more to their passion.

Being persistent doesn't mean that you have to work harder to get what you want. Instead, it means latching onto opportunities when they are placed in front of you and realizing that people entering and exiting your life are there for a reason and can help you get what you want. By becoming more sensitive to your needs and watching for subtle signs, they will appear and disappear quickly. You may identify that you can act on a sign immediately or the sign may just have been there to plant a seed that needs time to grow. However, when you are in the situation where what you need comes your way exactly when you need it, you need to be persistent and go after it. Be persistent in following up on the leads and the breadcrumbs that will be scattered ahead of you. Don't worry about it if the path of the breadcrumb trail looks like it is going nowhere or you cannot see where it ends. When you look behind you, the path will make sense and each piece of breadcrumb will have held information vital to your achieving your dream. Following the path may entail taking a risk and having faith in something you cannot see, but you need to trust your instincts and trust in your dream.

As I wrote in Chapter 5, I didn't follow-through with the dream I had as a teen to be a medical doctor. I took a very different career path but, over time, I began to realize that I needed to become persistent in providing myself with more opportunities to figure out what I wanted to be when I grew up. I applied on two separate occasions to different graduate programs, and was accepted. In both scenarios I got scared, believing that I could not balance working, life and school. I convinced myself that I just didn't have the time. So in each situation, I applied for an extension on my start date, but when the extensions ran out, so did my courage to execute on continuing my studies.

The idea of applying for the third time to a graduate program had been stewing in my mind for some time when I received an e-mail from one of the schools I had previously applied to, extended my start date then dropped out. The e-mail was a query as to whether I had given any thought to re-applying as they had room in the program I wanted and the start date was not far away. The timing was eerily perfect. I was experiencing an atypical lull in my professional life and had the capacity to take on something else. I jumped at the opportunity this time, ignoring the same fears I had before. I know now that all these actions lined up for a reason and that my persistence in wanting to pursue higher education was obtained as I acted on this e-mail. When I initiated taking graduate courses, at the time, I didn't think it was meant to lead to anything further academically. I saw it as getting another degree to give me more credibility in my current role, and set me up for potential part-time work as an instructor at a college or university.

Once I started to work on myself and define what it was that I wanted to do (around the same time that I decided to write this book), I saw my education goal being more than what it was. Re-connecting with my dream to write a book also brought me back to my dream of being a doctor. I had given up on medical school and had no passion to be a psychiatrist anymore, but I still wanted to help others and share knowledge with them. The breadcrumbs on the path lined up and I could see that they pointed to my graduate degree creating an opportunity that led to a PhD. I could be the doctor I wanted to be in a way I had not considered before.

With my new focus, I gained time, not only for family and myself but time to spend on going after my renewed dreams of writing a book and being a doctor. By giving up what I perceived as a lot, I gained so much more.

We as women need to be more persistent in dedicating time for ourselves. Mental and emotional stresses are so binding that we need to be persistent in finding time to relax and re-connect with ourselves in order to stay focused. I used to be horrible at this. Spending time on myself was pretty low on the priority list. Now I search out ways to find time for me.

When was the last time you took some time for yourself? A spa afternoon? A day at the beach? Curled up on the couch with a good book? Window-shopping? Cuddling with your kids? An hour at a coffee shop or bookstore by yourself? How are you persistent in finding time for yourself? If you are not finding time for yourself, why? What is stopping you?

My persistence to find a career that is fulfilling and rewarding has given me the time to work on the dreams I had when I was a teenager. I am now reconnecting with three of my childhood passions: writing, becoming a doctor and most importantly, helping others. My persistence in focusing on these goals has garnered me attention and networking opportunities that I did not imagine would come as a result going after what I wanted. Once I made the commitment to these goals, events began to fall into place. New people effortlessly came into my life who were able to share their knowledge and skill to help me fulfill my goals of being a writer and connecting with women and girls. Sharing pieces of information and acting upon ideas gained through networking opened up a world of opportunity and growth I could never have imagined. I became proficient in identifying the signs that appeared before me and following up on them as I began to visualize a rewarding career that left me fulfilled. Make no mistake, though, I still need to work on my persistence to ask others for help when I need it, when opportunities are coming into my life at the same time and I don't have the capacity to handle it all. Like all your skills, they need to be practiced over and over again before you can become an expert.

The persistence of taking risks with my career in order to find what would be personally fulfilling mentally and emotionally has brought me to this point in my life. The crossroads that I was at preceding my 40th birthday was the result of a journey to find myself that had taken me away from where I was meant to be but provided me with the stories, experiences and lessons to share. Once blended with faith and belief in myself, my persistence led me on to this unchartered career path of being a writer, connecting with women and girls and opening up a vortex of opportunities that now appears bottomless. A path of self-discovery that is allowing me to reach for and attain what I truly desired and dreamed about many years ago. I am once again at the foot of a new summit, looking up, armed with all the gear I need to make the climb, knowing that I will need something I don't yet have, but trusting that I will figure it out by being persistent. I am excited to make this climb and confident that, when I reach the top, there will be another summit waiting.

I am ready for the adventure.

What summit do you want to climb? What inspiration do you need to ignite your persistence to start or continue your journey and go after what you really want?

7

Learning From Others

Learning from others can be done from a multitude of informal and formal methods. Some learning opportunities are proactively planned and obvious, while others are spontaneous and subtle. In all the interactions we have with others and activities we -involve ourselves in, we are learning. We can learn something by ourselves that completely surprises us or rely on the expertise of somebody else to teach us when we have a knowledge gap. Within every situation, positive or not, there is a learning opportunity.

I had a multitude of opportunities to learn from many different coaches, teachers, bosses and peers across different learning scenarios, industries and company divisions. This has given me a wealth of experience in learning from others. As I reflect back on all of these leaders in my life, I can say that each has provided me with a learning opportunity whether I realized it at the time or not.

I played sports recreationally and competitively for a number of years. I have had supportive coaches with an endless supply of encouraging words and ones who paid little attention to me as I was not a star athlete. I have had teachers and leaders who were über-rigid in their thinking, allowing for little latitude or creative input into problem solving. I have had teammates who were focused on putting themselves first and others who were fantastic collaborators and cheerleaders whom I relied on to share fears and doubts and ask questions in confidence. I have come across a few negative souls who are stuck in a turbulent cycle of habits and paradigms.

What kind of coaches, peers, friends and people leaders have you had? What qualities and characteristics motivated you to want to work harder?

What de-motivated you? If you are a leader, which of your own attributes are you acutely aware of and make sure you exude in order to be the most effective? What leadership skills do you excel in? What leadership skills would you like to learn in order to help others and yourself grow personally and professionally?

My biggest transformational experience around learning from others came from when I was a student. One of my class assignments included a group project and I was assigned to work with a particular classmate and it did not go over well with me.

Although I had never worked with this classmate before, I respected the individual and their skills and knowledge, but I did not want to work with them, as I had a pre-conceived notion that our work philosophies would not mesh well based on what others had told me. For the first month of us working together, I was resistant to whatever ideas or activities that were put in front of me. The impact was a constant power struggle. Although project deadlines were being met, there was considerable emotional and mental baggage behind all of our interactions. It was an inefficient partnership that was wrought with passive-aggressive behaviors. One day towards the end of the semester, my classmate and I were having a rather civil discussion brainstorming ideas for our final project when somehow it turned into a tug-of-war of stubborn wills. At that moment, we both stopped, looked at each other and laughed as we both had finally reached our breaking points and all we could do was laugh at the situation. Following the laughter came an exceptionally honest discussion and it changed how I worked with this classmate. We went from battling wills to collaborating on ideas through the establishment of a powerful mastermind process, creating a shared vision for success. The tug-of-war turned into a symbiotic give-and-take where we learned from and supported each other.

What changed?

In my opinion, I was the cog in the wheel from the beginning as I entered the relationship with a negative attitude. I had a certain belief with no prior knowledge to support my feelings. My knowledge was based on what I had heard about the individual from others. Based on the experiences relayed by others, I created a paradigm in my mind of what it was going to be like to work with this person. As a result, I played out my role in the relationship exactly as I had scripted it, like a movie I should have won an Academy Award for as I was so convincing! I allowed my subconscious thoughts to control the behavior that caused my actions to perpetuate in a way that continued to validate my belief I could not work with this class-mate. What I learned during the straightforward tete-a-tete was that my actions caused the construction of barriers that were not limited to just me. There were three sets of barriers built; one around me, one around my classmate and one between us. In a truly transformational experience, we broke down our barriers and re-built our perceptions and beliefs from a blank slate. Moving forward, our partnership flourished. When the project finished I was sad to see the partnership end but happy to grow the friendship that had started.

I realize now that I made the mistake of being emotionally shutdown and negative to a situation built on false belief. I am thankful I was able to come to my senses because, if not, I would have missed out on so many valuable learning opportunities. My classmate and I mentored each other as our academic backgrounds were different but had transferable skills. Learning this knowledge became critical as I continued along in my career as it was knowledge that I needed and relied on in various business scenar-ios. Learning these skills became critical in my professional development and during the writing and marketing of this book. From this experience I learned that sometimes my ego needs to take a step back, to not enter into relationships with pre-conceived beliefs, to focus on the positive instead of negative thoughts and to find the learning opportunity that exists in any situation, including those that at first are not desirable. I have learned that putting out negative behavior will only bring negativity back my way. I am not always going to get what I want or have control over every situation. Isn't that what a parent teaches a child? I know I do!

What I am now able to realize is that I need to open myself up, relinquish control and hand over my faith so that I am more comfortable being open to defining learning moments from others, as the knowledge shared may be invaluable even if I do not realize it at the time.

Have you ever been in a situation where events matched what you believed they would be? When you were positive about a situation or person and the outcome matched that positive vision? How much did you learn? Or a negative perception of a person or situation and the outcome matched the negative vision? How much did you learn in this negative situation? How much of your own personal biases and beliefs do you feel impacted the outcome in each type of situation?

I am thankful for the array of personal and professional opportunities that have provided me with the ability to learn from others on how to develop a vision, the different methods to communicate and gain buy-in on the vision and finally, the strategies to execute in order to gain results and move towards the vision.

Each coach and leader in my career have possessed different styles when sharing their vision, but all styles utilized tools that brought the vision to life and gave it shape so that those reading or hearing it could visualize it. Coaches would pull out the wipe-board and draw out a particular play or strategy for the team to visualize and act on with the desire to meet the vision of scoring a goal (or preventing one). Business leaders would develop slides using pictures to illustrate goals and display results against the goals. A positive outcome of this book would be for women and girls to learn the knowledge, skills and abilities to identify what they truly want in life and find a way to visualize it and write it down so others can see it too. For women to leverage the empowerment they feel within themselves to guide a girl in her emotional development of self, and cause a ripple effect of learning through reflection and storytelling, helping girls to believe in themselves. I learned that it is easier to go after a dream or desire when you (and others!) are so passionate and in love with something that you are able to create a vision in your mind that can be translated onto paper or into spoken word so precisely that others can also see and feel what the vision is.

Your dream could be saving money for a trip or a new house, increasing your sales, improving your communication skills, or getting over a fear of public speaking. Any dream that is in your mind can be translated into visible form through a picture or words. Look back at the desires and dreams you have and wrote down back in Chapter 4. Ask yourself if you can visualize the desire or dream as it is written down. What further details can be added to add detail to the desire? Is there a finite time when you want to go after or achieve your desires by? If you learn more effectively through pictures and are a visual learner, then try and draw a picture based on the desires you have written down. No journalism or artistic skills are needed!

During the writing of this book, I learned how to visualize what I wanted my end result to be. Experts entered my life who were able to teach and nurture my intuitive abilities, to explain in explicit details how my success made me feel and what it looked like in very granular detail. Being able to visualize the completion of this book and its resulting success motivated me to continue to put my thoughts and stories onto paper and reinforced my belief that I could write a book. It then went further to guide me in knowing that it would have a positive impact not just on my life, but on the lives of women and girls. How often have you caught yourself daydreaming of having more than you have now? That you could see yourself someplace exotic or owning certain things. That is visualizing! What you dream about can be turned into reality. For me, learning how to visualize was inspiring and provided the crux I would return to when I needed the creative energy and focus to finish this book and fulfill my dream.

When a vision can be seen or put into words, it can make it easier to identify what actions are needed in order to achieve the vision. I want you to be able to think about what you want; to create a vision and a picture that tangible actions can be made against. The vision that is developed will more than likely identify the gaps in your knowledge or skills that you will need to fill via learning from others. If you have a big dream that involves something you have never done before, it means that you will need to acquire new knowledge and learning in order to do it, or find an expert to do it for you.

As I started to craft the knowledge and skills I needed in order to start moving towards my dream, I became more knowledgeable and confident in what I was doing and more adept at being able to identify the granular details of what was required and who I needed to become connected with in order to acquire what was critical to my dream and necessary to expedite my journey. What I learned along the way through my mentor's persistence was to trust that what, how or who I needed to learn from would show up when I needed it and at the right time. With this lesson drilled into me on a continuous basis, I began to be much better at trusting in my faith that something I had no tangible proof existed or was real would actually come to fruition.

In order for me to achieve my dream of writing a book and helping women and girls, I had a lot of learning to do, as this was something I had never attempted before in my life.

To support and guide my learning, I became skilled in my ability to network (something I was not previously adept at doing) and surrounded myself with a powerful coalition of men and women who were experts in their designated fields, from authors to human resource specialists, marketing gurus, teachers, health & wellness specialists to personal coaches and motivational speakers. I collaborated on knowledge procured from these individuals in order to write and publish this book. I needed to source out respected individuals I could trust to secure the knowledge and skills I required to continue to move forward in achieving what I wanted.

I am not a marketing expert nor did I know the first thing about how to publish a book, so I met with individuals who were at various stages in their own publishing journey (from working on a manuscript to already being an international best-seller) to learn from their personal experiences and discover where I needed to perform more research.

Should I self-publish or go with a traditional publisher? What were the current manuscript requirements and trends in the book industry? How should I develop my brand and blog about it? How could I create a book cover? What are efficient and cost-effective distribution and sales tactics? All this was a foreign language until I worked with experts to learn more so that I knew where to take control, what tasks I could accomplish and where to let the experts remain in control. I got much better at making decisions about what I could or could not do as I gained knowledge and confidence around the process of turning my dream into a reality.

Using a coalition of peers and colleagues is an effective method for learning from others, and it has the added benefit of being a relationship whereby you can reciprocate the learning cycle by sharing your knowledge. I really like the idea of the learning circle and learning from others in any type of situation. An atypical situation, where I have found success in learning form others, has come from asking others for their opinion and feedback. In school we would get unsolicited feedback from teachers on how we performed on a test or an assignment, with the outcome of the feedback aligning to measuring the result of an action via a grade. I had some teachers who would provide a plethora of written results in addition to the grade, and others who would just provide a grade with little to no feedback, constructive or not. The absence of words written with a red pen, in my experience, meant that the work I provided met the teachers' expectations and resulted in a good grade.

How do you feel about receiving feedback from others? What about giving feedback? What kind of feedback do you give when asked? Do you decline to give feedback to others because you do not know what to say or are afraid of how the receiver will feel if it is not positive?

The thing about feedback is that as uncomfortable as it may be, it is a powerful method for learning from others. As daunting as it sounds, if you solicit feedback from people you respect and who are genuinely interested in supporting your personal or professional development, you will receive constructive, positive feedback on where your opportunities and future successes lie. If you focus on feedback as a negative state that creates the emotion you will need to overcome in order to create a positive action. An exponential leap would be required to move to the equivalent positive state and typically will not motivate you to want to make a change, even if it meant you would succeed!

Remember, feedback is based on the perceptions of somebody else and it is what it is. With feedback, there might be many tangible items you can take action on or there might be a single, but critical, piece of information you need to fill a learning gap. The great thing about feedback is that you can accept it into your subconscious or you can reject it. That power and ability lies with you. Unfortunately what usually happens, and I am guilty on this, is that I do not reject feedback that is not supportive and I take it personally and create a negative emotion out of it instead of accepting it for what it is and keeping myself positive in my emotions and thoughts of myself.

The content of feedback can sometimes be hard to receive, especially if you are passionate about something and the person giving you feedback does not share this passion. The "how" around feedback is equally, if not more important than "what" the feedback was. Have you ever received feedback from somebody who identified that you had a lot of opportunities for improvement but left you feeling positive about what efforts you had made and motivated you to want to take action on the opportunities? How did that person convey the feedback to you? How did their communication style engage you to learn from what they said to you?

Sometimes, feedback could feel like a punch to the gut. Sound familiar? Passive-aggressive or simply aggressive styles always made me cringe, even when the feedback being delivered was positive! Sometimes feedback was delivered like an undercover superhero, with words cloaked in disguise and the intentions or messages hidden. Positive feedback would be completely missed as it could not be construed out from the emotion and the tone of the voice used to deliver the feedback.

Sometimes learning from others is not obvious or easy; messages can be hidden or blatantly put in front of you. The act of learning from the adult learning perspective requires a level of "what's in it for me" or "how is this going to benefit me" attitude if learning opportunities are being sought out or involuntarily provided. When asking for feedback, information sourcing is driving the learning opportunity which, in return, will influence the retaining and use of the learning material and motivating one to search through a proverbial jungle of content to find the knowledge needed. If you really want or need to learn from others, you will do what it takes to find the right person to learn from and decipher the message you need from the information supplied to you.

As I grew in my confidence as a leader, I would find situations where I could incorporate giving feedback to others, and provide a safe environment for others to give me feedback in a direct manner so that no searching for hidden treasures of knowledge was required. As an advocate for using critical reflection as a learning tool, I would regularly ask team members to think back 30 days and identify something they did and were proud of or that they felt they did well. This was a tool to get them used to self-identifying their own achievements, being proud of their accomplishments and providing themselves with feedback as a way to learn from what they did well.

What is something you have done in the last 30 days that you are proud of? Why did you choose this example? What can you learn from this example that you can apply to something else in your life?

Other reflection activities I incorporated into discussions was give others the opportunity to provide me with feedback on something they saw me do in the last 30 days that they appreciated or liked, or something that I could do differently in order to support their needs.

The purpose of me asking for feedback was threefold:
1) For me to learn what the needs were for people I supported in a variety of roles,
2) For me to learn if I was effectively supporting these needs and,
3) To provide others with a safe environment in which to learn how to give feedback and respond to questions regarding the feedback.

I learned from feedback that it was the small things I did that were appreciated. I helped others to be comfortable managing upwards as I would be given great ideas on how I could be more proficient in my workday or a resourceful leader. Because feedback was provided in a professional manner and I was asking for it in order to support others better (the "what's in it for me" requirement), I was more open and motivated to take action on the feedback. It also helped me to believe in myself and validate that I knew what I was doing as some days my confidence in my skills and abilities could be stretched thin.

In order for you to achieve any dream or vision, whether business or personal, you will need to learn from others in order to obtain a knowledge or skill for you to do something yourself, or learn from experts that you should leave some things up to them. If you are expecting to conquer the world on your own, how hard do you think that would be? How long do you think it would take? By sourcing out people and asking questions and learning from them, not only will you acquire knowledge and skills you probably did not realize you would have, but you will have significantly decreased the overall effort that you need to exert in order to conquer your fears or learning gaps to achieve your dream.

Throughout this book, I wrote of my desire to help others. This may be through some women learning from mistakes that I have made (and described in these chapters), it may be through generating further ideas through positive, constructive feedback. I want to learn how to best support the learning of others, and if feedback is offered with the best of intentions, it will be. If laying out my vulnerabilities within the pages of this book creates a learning opportunity for someone else, then I have achieved my desire of helping others.

I learned so much from others during the writing of this book, and am encouraged and motivated to see what else I can learn as this journey takes me down new and exciting paths.

What I am confident in is that, when I reflect back on what I have learned up to this point, I will be able to see how it has all been connected, and of the immense value that can be gained from the experience of learning from others.

8

Surrounding Yourself With the Best

There are a number of different types of friendships, and how you act and behave in each friendship is based on the value of the role you play. The value may be limited to what you need from the friendship, or it may be diminished and starved due to your perception of the value you can provide to the friendship. If you feel you cannot provide value to others, then you are limiting your own potential for unbounded friendship. Your belief in how you can build, initiate and provide value to a relationship can directly impact your ability to procure and sustain value-added relationships. How you believe in yourself impacts who you attract and who you can retain around you.

What type of people do you want to surround yourself with?

Surface-level friendships can occur anywhere; from your school days to your workplace to the teams you or your children are a part of. Sometimes you have the freedom of choice whether to engage in a friendship or acquaintanceship with someone, but sometimes you do not. If you do not have a choice, you need to figure out how to make the best of a situation. Easier said than done, right? We've all been there. Polite smiles. Idle chitchat to fill the void of silence. It is a part of being in society and interacting with others, and for the most part, I can say that I have had only had a few negative experiences. I have to be honest too, in that I was that person who was uncomfortable with the idle chitchat. I used to feel awkward in groups of people I did not know well. I had felt I could not provide value to conversations, so I would not speak up. So I can totally admit that I was both a victim and contributor to non-value friendships. The result was that nobody asked me questions or got to know me. I kept people closed off as to whom I was. Although I truly wanted to be part of the conversations around me, my belief that I was awkward prevented me from taking risks and speaking up. I always admired people who had the gift of the gab and could spark a conversation with anyone, anytime.

Fortunately, as my confidence has grown, I have learned that I can change how I see myself and transform that feeling of awkwardness into confidence and extroversion. I seek out opportunities to initiate conversations and connections with people I do not know and am continually surprised at how open and accepting they can be. I used to be afraid of rejection. Now I take chances with the belief that my olive branch will be accepted. This is a work in progress as I become more comfortable and experienced in starting conversations, and I can be honest in saying that awkwardness does creep back into controlling me but at least now I am aware of it and know that I can reject that feeling. I continually make a conscious effort to be in a state of confidence in the effort to turn surface-level friendships into value-added ones. I realized I missed out on getting to know some amazing and wonderful people by being closed off, and know I was sometimes perceived by others as snobby and cold.

Then you have value-added friendships. These are friendships that you are emotionally involved in, that you have a stake in and that you have a connection to. Valuable friendships are not bound by the time you have known somebody. Their strength comes from an elevated, shared emotional connection or intimate experience. They are not measured in quantity but in quality. These are the friends who will support you during your best and worst times, and that you will support when called upon. Distance and time do not cause the friendship to falter but ensures that you place even more value on the time that you do spend connecting.

A good friend builds you up and supports you, no matter what. I have learned over the years that people come in and out of your life for different periods of time, for different reasons. And sometimes friendships have surpassed their expiration date but you still linger long after it has gotten stale. Why is that? Is it sentimental value? You don't want to be seen as negative as you cut ties or have difficulty saying good-bye. What do you do when friendships that were once value-added are no longer providing you with satisfaction or positive support? When words of encouragement slowly and subtly turn to venom, hidden in passive-aggressive humor?

A friend of mine and I met on the first day of a new school year. He had just moved to my school from across the city. It took some time but we eventually warmed up to each other. Through our academic years we both had our challenges but we supported each other with words and acts of encouragement. We had a lot in common going through school. We both wanted to have careers in the medical field and, as such, we were in all the science classes together. We both experienced tribulations in our respective post-secondary careers, but we both finished. He on time and me a year late, but we finished nonetheless. After graduation we both started out on the next phase of adult life. Decades after, even as we both became entrenched in growing our professional careers in different cities, we managed to stay in touch on a regular basis with both of us being equal participants.

Within the first five years of my career, an amazing professional opportunity was presented to me and I accepted it. I was excited so naturally I called my friend to share the news. The reception that I received, though, was not even close to what I was expecting.

"Bitch."

Like the hockey arena scenario I shared earlier, I vividly remember this moment. There was a hint of humor in his voice as he said the word but, in its undertone, it seemed to be subtly laced with something else. It definitely was not said in a joking manner and I could tell he was not happy for me. I managed to finish the conversation. I was excited with my news and ignored the comment though remaining consciously aware that the conversation had become one-dimensional. After I hung up I thought about the comment that he had made. The tone of the conversation after I shared my news was definitely different than before.

Unsure of why there was a change in attitude, but not wanting to make a big deal out of it, I sought my friend out for business advice as I was engaging in this new opportunity and he had experience in the venture I was diverting into. As a creative person and being business savvy, his advice and mentoring was welcome to me as I was new in the role. He answered my questions but I found the responses missing in granular detail. There was a lack of excitement and engagement in his communication with me that was atypical for him. I extended an offer to connect face-to-face and we met, but he was distant and our visit was much shorter than usual and our conversation lacked depth.

Whenever I attempted to broach the subject to ask if I had done something wrong, he would cut me off and our conversation would end soon after that. As I became successful in my new opportunity, my conversations with him became shorter, less frequent and always initiated by me. With no feedback from him about whether he was intentionally being distant because of my career success (his career had not changed since graduation), I made the decision that our friendship needed to be a two-way collaboration or it could not continue. I no longer had the emotional capacity or patience to worry about what I had done to make him behave the way he was. It was a one-sided effort, resulting in a diminished value in what the friendship once was. So one day, I made the decision to not initiate conversation. And I waited. After a year with no response, I took the absence of any kind of communication (including no Christmas card) as validation that our friendship had run its course.

Could I have put more effort into saving the relationship? Probably. Did I think it was worth the effort? At the time, no. As I reflect on it now, I still believe the answer is no. I had tried. He remained closed off. You can't force somebody to face emotions they are not ready to admit to and deal with. Many people are not comfortable with reflecting on what they might have done wrong. In this scenario, maybe our friendship had run its course and my friend just didn't care to continue on with our relationship. Have I thought since about "what could have been" if I put in more effort? Yes, but I have no guilt over what I did or did not do.

It was unfortunate that friendship with him did not last long enough for our children to meet, but the negativity and lack of support or happiness for me in my achievements were emotionally draining. If there are two people in a friendship, there should be two people being supportive. Only half of a dyad being supportive causes a negative imbalance in the polarity of the friendship and I could no longer see how this friendship was helping me to grow positively as a person.

As I have learned, witnessed and experienced, in order for you to be successful in any aspect of your life you need to surround yourself with people who have a genuine interest in your personal growth and development, be it your partner/spouse or your friends. They are people who, after whatever length of absence, can pick up the phone or meet in person and have an effortless conversation. Your true value-added friendships are not counted in social media but are counted from your memories. Positive people around you increase the positive vibration you feel and exude which then plays out into your actions and behaviors and sets you up for personal and professional success. I continue to learn that I need to politely disassociate myself from the negative influences of people in my life. Negativity has a powerful impact on how you feel, think and behave. To stay focused on being positive requires the elimination of negative vibrations from others that pull you down by either not associating with them or being able to consciously arm yourself against the negativity coming at you.

Think about the kinds of friendships you have now versus those you had when you were younger. What are the differences? Are there any similarities? Have you change your circle of friends as you have grown older? What was the reason you ended a friendship you once valued? What value do you place on your friendships now? How are you being a supportive friend now versus what you did when you were younger? How have you changed in order to best support your friends?

I had a miscarriage a number of years ago. The resulting memories are the most painful I have experienced to date. I spent months feeling guilty and that I had done something wrong to cause the loss of my baby. At the time, I hadn't shared the news with many people beyond my closest circle of friends due to the personal nature of it.

The day after my miscarriage there was an engagement party for a good friend that I had previously RSVP'd to. The party planner called me on the day of the event to confirm my numbers for the reservation and my husband, who took the call, hesitated. I had pretty much relegated myself to either my bed or the couch, in and out of tears, and hammering myself with questions and scenarios about what I had done, what I could have done, and what I should have done, believing that I could have somehow prevented the miscarriage. My husband explained the situation to the planner who understood and empathized as she too had suffered a miscarriage. She shared her experience with me through my husband as I was in no condition to communicate but was open to hearing about her experience. She convinced me to come out to the event, using her empathy and her experience that being around people who cared for me and being outside of the four walls I was surrounding myself with could help me through my grieving process. Believing her and putting faith in her experience, we went to the party. While we did not stay late, I was glad I went. My friends knew what it had taken for me to come out and they provided immense support. They respected the fact that I was not partaking in the lively conversations and I encouraged them to not dampen their celebration. Celebrating life was helping to keep my feelings elevated.

Surrounding yourself with the best people can, even in grief and sorrow, lift your spirits or at least keep them level. Supportive friends do not just watch you in a situation, they jump into the trenches with you, they fight alongside you and they celebrate with you. You all grow stronger. They can take a tragic situation and give you the faith and belief that you will make it through, perhaps wounded and scarred, but ultimately healed and wiser from the experience.

After my healing process had begun, I started to slowly share my news and, once again, was astonished at the support and sharing of stories related to the same tragedy from other women. Reflecting back on that period of time in my life, it was the positive sharing of emotionally-charged stories from women who could empathize with my situation that provided me with the comfort and the safety net to help me heal and work through my grieving process.

I believe that what really helped me the night I went out was the fact that I had a group of friends around me. The power of positive thought can be amplified when in a group. Have you ever experienced being in a group situation, either socially or in a school or work team, when the energy emitted from the group can be felt? When you feel a positive vibration and the group to be connected in the same single vision: to spend time with each other? It is an amazing feeling. In a collective vibration with a group, your own experience and sense of being in the moment is heightened, and your creative factors are more sensitive and open to learning, both through the stories being told as well as your own process of reminiscing.

I was reminded of the impact of the power of a group when I recently walked into a local coffee establishment on a beautiful, but cool, fall weekend to sit down, read and warm myself up with a hot beverage while, taking advantage of time in-between dropping off and picking up my kids from their activities. As soon as I entered, my intuition kicked in and I could feel multiple sets of eyes on me. I glanced to the side and sure enough there was a group of individuals sitting together that I knew. I went over to chat a bit before finding a seat to focus on my book. Even after I put in my ear buds and started up my music, I could hear the laughter and muddled conversations from this group. They were sharing stories and their thoughts with each other and, as a group, they were connected. A common thread connected them. Through their years of friendship they connected through history, and they evidently still supported each other, enjoying their time with each other. Even after decades of friendship, it is amazing how relationships can continue to evolve as you each grow as individuals and continually bring new insights, perceptions and thoughts to each other, resulting in a continuous avenue for learning from others.

Like convincing me to come out to dinner that evening, supportive friends know when to push you when you have created boundaries (valid and artificial) and walls for yourself. They challenge your thoughts and perceptions, your wisdom and your knowledge to aid in your personal development for the long term.

I used to have a serious hang-up regarding my age. After turning 30, I believed it was downhill from there. It was then a countdown in the number of days until I was 40. This was all based on my perception that, even at 30, I was not yet doing what I was truly meant to do. That at 30, I had not accomplished much, even though I was professionally successful and had given birth to my first child, a blessed addition to my personal success. I hadn't yet reached a level of success I was content with. But if you had asked me at 30 what I wanted to be, I still would not have been able to give you a concise answer. All I could identify was that by 40, I wanted to have a "manager" title. That was pretty much the extent of my 10-year succession and development plan that I spoke of in a prior chapter.

As the years went on, I avoided birthdays which as much vigor as I could. Having children made that less possible, however, as they enjoyed celebrating it when they were old enough. It made me feel better for much of my 30s that my children thought I was much younger than I was) and I did not feel the need to correct them. When my son was old enough to add, we were talking about the ages of my siblings and he figured out that it didn't make sense that my younger sister was older than me. At that point, I admitted that I was not the age he thought I was (19), though I still limited my age to 29. Closer to the truth but still not the truth.

I do have fond memories of a couple of my birthdays during my 30s because of how friends tried everything they could to influence my negative perception of my age, to get me to laugh at myself and just accept the day for what it was. From baking for me to conspiring with my husband to throw me a surprise party. A few, not wanting to push the boundaries too much, took me out to a lovely dinner with "just the girls".

I did cross the fence on those birthdays that day and glanced at what the other side looked like. I even slithered down the fence a couple of times and stood on the ground, finding comfort in the knowledge that these wonderful people thought enough of me to try and change my stubborn perception. That they trusted the realms of our friendship enough to push my limits to increase my comfort zone, even if just temporarily, without me getting angry. They were nice birthdays. Good friends challenge you and are willing to take calculated risks with the relationship as a participant, not an observer, to support you and help you to grow and learn about yourself.

Do you have a friend or group of friends that you continuously seem to learn from? What kinds of experiences are they having and sharing for you to learn from? What is it about their experiences that you enjoy learning about the most? Have you told your friends recently that you enjoy listening to them and absorbing their wisdom?

The closer I got to 40, the greater had been my desire to avoid my birthday because the career and personal choices I had made were still not providing me with feelings of fulfillment, the entitlement I desired or a balanced lifestyle. I had been vocal in the months leading up to my birthday that I would not be in the country for the dreaded date unless "something" required me to stay home. Sure enough, the universe was determined for me to face my fear of age head-on as one of my children had an important event to him that got booked on my birthday. Of course! Even the universe would not let me avoid dealing with my paradigms.

When I think about it now, with all the cultural hoopla around turning 40, the time to change my thinking about myself and my current life environment could not have come at a more perfectly planned moment. On my birthday, I took the day off work to spend it on myself, something I had not been able to do in a long time. I went to a spa in the morning to be pampered and relax, which the esthetician said I did not do very well. After the spa I headed off to lunch with my friend who had planted that seed of change in my mind many months before. We talked about my age paradigm, my difficulty in relaxing, my continued lack of balance and my fears around how it was impacting my marriage and relationship with my kids. We focused our conversation on my need to create time to devote to my family and myself.

So much was out of balance in my life at 40 that I did not want to spend my next 40 years struggling to find balance. I knew my marriage would not last and was all too aware that my kids' impressionable years were now when they still needed, and wanted, me. This friend was not afraid to have an uncomfortable conversation with me. No topic or question was taboo. She was not afraid to ask difficult questions of me, or to point out that how I thought about myself was both the cause and only solution to my need for a better life balance. She did not judge but she did push me out of my comfort zone to look at the reality of my life and myself. She was right and didn't say anything that I had not already said to myself before but was afraid to utter out loud to anybody other than close confidants. And once again, a seed was planted.

I learned much from that one lunch conversation about myself. The humorous part was that I learned I was not as good an actress as I thought I was. My displeasure with my life and the stress of the imbalance was more obvious to people than I had hoped. It had subconsciously become part of my demeanor. I knew that my "real" self showed at home. When I arrived there I could not carry on my act any longer. I was exhausted to the point where I needed "downtime" by myself before I could partake in activities. So my family experienced the negative effects of my exhaustion after I performed all day long. When out with friends, I kept my guard up (or at least I thought I did) but learned that I could only hide my inner emotions and feelings for so long before they started to show through physical and emotional changes that the outside world could see. I learned that "fake it until you make it" was temporary for me, and that at some point in time the wiring in my brain wouldn't handle the overload of stress on it caused by my constant fighting to control my emotions and my body wanting to snap. A friend had taken a leap of faith to leave her own flourishing career that she enjoyed and was completely satisfied with in order to search out even bigger opportunities and a gratification she could have never imagined. I learned that she was able to make the exorbitant leap without looking down due to the support of her family and a network of close friends. If she did it, could I also learn how to do it too in order to seek out personal gratification? Hmm. What was that again? I couldn't remember.

Are you the award-winning actress that you think you are? Have you ever put on a performance in order to hide how you were truly feeling? Who was the audience that witnessed the award-winning performance--and who got the "real" performance? What was the driving force behind each performance? How is your behavior impacting your relationships with others? How is it impacting you going after your dream?

For years I had been having conversations with friends about job satisfaction. You know how it is, you get together at a dinner party and the conversation quickly starts with "How are you?", "How are things going?", "How are the kids?", and "What's new at work?" I was always amazed to hear that quite a few of my friends were completely happy and fulfilled with their chosen careers, even after many years. They were not able to relate to me when I shared with them my overall neutral attitude surrounding my job. They could not understand how I continued to work at something I was not passionate about. I could not understand how they could be so passionate about what they did. When I look at these friends, I can reflect and see that they all had something in common; they started off in one direction with their schooling and careers, and early-on made the decision to switch to doing something that they were passionate about. And they did not regret making the switch even though it set them back financially or they had to start their academic careers all over again. They took a risk to change their journeys in order to be true to what they believed in and pursue a career that fit their personal beliefs and what they truly wanted to do. They all now worked in careers where they served and helped others, and took pride in their abilities to do so.

I used to be so jealous of them for knowing what they were passionate about and then taking the actions they needed to get them to where they needed to be. Now, because I have also stepped back and given myself the time to reflect on what I truly desire to do and go after what I am passionate about, I can feel, experience and relate to what it is has been like for my friends to truly enjoy their careers.

Within days of foraging forward towards my new life, compliments began to come from friends and acquaintances that I looked healthier, seemed more relaxed and smiled a lot more. The physical toll of the lifestyle I had led was retracting and I started to feel better on the inside, which was reflective of how I began to look on the outside. I reminded people of the person I was years ago, before I allowed corporate ladder-climbing, kids and additional responsibilities take control of who I was. I am glad that they remembered the person I used to be as I had forgotten about her. I was me, only better.

If it wasn't for surrounding myself with great friends, I would not have been able to make the leap to resigning from my job. Their continuous encouragement and reminders that growing my career as a mother trumped any corporate career growth helped me do it. My friends even supported me by looking out for jobs for me that aligned with my desires and dreams. I continue to be empowered by these amazing women and men because the support they have given me makes me want to be the person they believe I am.

I am eternally grateful to my friends who have stuck around and remained my friends despite my lack of presence (physically, emotionally, electronically or virtually) for many years. They understood my desire to be a working mother and now understand my need for time and dedication to my family and to me. They do not chastise me for making the mistake of not dedicating time for myself and for creating the unfulfilling life I had been living. At times, they still could not believe I finally took the risk, but they supported me in my progression of a new lifestyle that was more balanced and included time for me. I am now more proficient at making the conscious effort to spend time with friends. I have weekly standing dates with some of them. Some I connect with frequently via social media and electronic communications that have resulted in the added benefit of me increasing my prowess and technical skill with social media! Something I used to ignore as much as possible!

I have learned that to help me stay happy and positive, I need to surround myself with people who are positive, optimistic and happy with themselves and their lives and are able to be truly supportive and positive of others. I truly believe that positivity from one person yields positivity in others, including positive attitudes. By reflecting on the impact of surrounding myself with the best of friends, I realized that I did not need nor want the leeching of negative attitudes around me.

Surrounding yourself with the best means that you need to be able to be comfortable in how you deal with the negative people around you. I learned the impact that negative people had on my ability to remain positive and persistent in pursuing my desires and dreams. Unless you live in a bubble though, contact with negative people or situations within your daily travels is a given. By now understanding that negativity is relative to a person's own thoughts and behaviors, I work hard to continually balance a negative thought or behavior with an equivalent positive thought or behavior. How somebody responds to others or a situation is relative to their own mood, habits and paradigms. In my case, I had to learn to remove emotion from how people responded to me, and conversely, how I responded to others. Where I used to take a response personally, I can now block that emotion from impacting me. While practicing this process is still new to me, the benefits are worth it as I can avoid being pulled into a negative vibration and can control my ability to positively respond to a negative situation instead of reacting negatively.

Can you remember a time when you were in a negative situation? How did you feel in the situation? Did the people around you respond or react to the situation? How did you respond? What habits or paradigms caused you to respond in the manner that you did? Could you have responded differently?

Surrounding myself as much as possible with the best and most positive people makes dealing with the negative or non-value-added people and situations much easier to tolerate and harder to get sucked into. I have become more consciously aware that, in order to remove negativity from around me, I need to combat it by responding positively. To react to a situation or person is negative. To respond to a situation or person relies on the use of self-control, a leadership quality that can be used use to get a point across while still being respectful of others and oneself. This is not easy. It can be difficult to remove yourself from a negative situation or person without offending, but this is where my belief in who and where I want to be needs to be stronger than my fear of what somebody will think of me.

Who you choose to surround yourself with is a reflection of yourself. The people surrounding you can either stand beside you or lift you up, or they can hold you down. They can teach you about yourself or keep your sense of self in bondage.

Look around at who you have surrounded your life with. What is it telling you about yourself?

9

Making Decisions

One of my favorite things to do is go grocery shopping. I am continually awestruck by the variety of foods available in the aisles and the ingenuity of food packaging on the shelves. The grocery aisle, however, was also where I used to have the most difficult time making a decision.

It might not seem like a difficult thing to do but some days I would debate with myself over which can of Cream of Mushroom soup to buy. Should I stick with the loyal brand or go with the generic option? Are any on sale? What is the best size for the dollar value? Go with low sodium or low-fat because it is better for you but the kids will notice and complain? Do I really need this $1 can of soup this week as it was not officially on the grocery list? Yep – I can honestly say that I have had this inner dialogue over picking up a can of soup and putting it into my cart. I cannot count the number of times I reached for an item on the shelf only to pull my hand back and divert it to another option only to then re-divert it back to the original choice. Sometimes I found it very difficult to make a decision on something that should have, theoretically, been easy to do. I'm sure that I provided some level of entertainment to anyone who happened to be in the same aisle as me, watching me contemplate a decision over and over again, my body a visual display of the battle going on in my mind.

The ability to make a confident decision is developed from a multitude of skills and enhanced by personal experience, sometimes trial and error, and importantly, our mistakes. I have been the primary grocery shopper in my household for 15 years so I have the skills and experience in order to make an informed decision on the best can of soup to buy, but what was happening to minimize my ability to make a decision?

Being able to make value-added and efficient decisions is a critical action, as it will set into motion a multitude of reactions. Now, buying the wrong can of soup one time will not necessarily have detrimental effects on my physical or financial well-being (barring any unknown food safety concerns at the time of purchase), but jumping into a high-risk business or financial agreement like buying a house, accepting a promotion or leaving a job will play out into reactive events that have deeper consequences and impact if a wrong decision is made.

What are the types of decisions that you find difficult to make? Is there a common theme? Is a lack of knowledge or skill the root cause of the indecisiveness or is it something else? What are other barriers stop you from making decisions?

Sometimes you have to make a decision with little or no knowledge of what the reaction to your decision-making action will be. You don't have all the data. Over my career, I had to make numerous decisions based on limited data or not knowing what the impact would be. I could make these decisions based on my experience or by using the combined minds and experience of others. Sometimes using others to help make a decision added layers of complexity, additional follow-ups and took more time. Other times, the combining of minds was magical and decisions could be made quickly and what seemed to be effortlessly.

How do you learn to make decisions? What are the decisions you made where the reactions were positive? As I said in the preface, give yourself credit for your good decisions and action! Have you made any decisions that you regretted? If so, what was the regret? If you could go back in time and tell yourself what to do, what decision would you change and why? And you can't just say "I don't know." If you feel you made a wrong decision there must be a "why" behind it.

Making decisions is harder when there is more than just you involved. The decision then becomes about the balance between the minds involved. When my husband and I were renewing our mortgage together for the first time, I wanted a variable mortgage with a lower rate but a higher risk because of fluctuations in the market but my husband was set on a fixed mortgage where payments were known for the next five years with zero risk of them increasing over that period. We discussed our reasons for how we came up with our decision and why we felt that our individual choice was the best option for the family. After many discussions, talking to friends and a mortgage broker we went with the fixed mortgage. Neither I nor others that we talked to could change his mind. His comfort level with fixed mortgages was rooted in what he had experienced and heard of growing up. I too had grown up in a household that took a conservative approach to finances, but I was open to making a decision with a higher risk because I wanted to save money. He stood firm in his belief and comfort and I knew that I could not change his decision, so I changed mine. No big deal, but the reaction to that decision was that we were not able to take advantage of the lower rates and missed out on saving thousands of dollars over the five-year period.

At the time we were financially stable enough not to be dependent on every dollar we spent, but when we had to renew after five years was up, the difference between what we still owed in the mortgage versus what we would have owed if we had been on a variable mortgage spoke to my husband's growing desire to keep our money in our own pockets versus his diminishing fear of the risk associated with a variable mortgage. So negotiating our renewal and going with variable mortgage was an easy decision for both of us to make. The "what's in it for me" question was the driver for my husband to become more knowledgeable and comfortable with the risk of changing our type of mortgage. Although I had wanted to go with the variable mortgage the first time around, I could not force my husband to make a decision he was not comfortable with. He needed knowledge, an increased awareness of his desire to keep our money working for us, not somebody else, and abundance before he could be comfortable changing his decision.

I haven't always made the best decisions and, reflecting back on events, I can identify that the root cause of my inability to make right decisions was because I was not confident in myself and did not believe I could follow through and meet the expectations of the reactions that would result if I had made the better decision.

Opportunities to change jobs and careers were presented to me over my career that I declined because I was scared of the unknown or not confident that I had the skills to do the job well. These were usually jobs similar to or along the same description as what I was doing at the time. But I dared not stray from what I was comfortable with. I'm pretty sure that I ticked off the recruiters and companies who I had received job offers from only to decline them. Long commutes, unaligned salary expectations, too little vacation time, thinking that maybe the grass would not be greener somewhere else or the exhaustion of back-and-forth negotiations resulted in me over-thinking the situation and becoming worried about changing jobs. This caused me to lose belief in myself and the results I could achieve and become fearful that I was not the right candidate for the job. I would then make the decision to decline the job offer. I would become uncomfortable seeing myself and believing I had the skills that another company was able to see in me. What if I disappointed them? What if I disappointed myself? What if I was just that award-winning actress I talked about earlier? Intuitively, I wondered if the job was really what I wanted. If it wasn't what I wanted, was it fair to the employer for me to go work for them? These were hard decisions, and uncomfortable ones, but I made them. And to be honest, I felt horrible after making them. As a people-pleaser, I didn't want to disappoint anybody. But I ended up being disappointed in myself. Reflecting back, I'm glad that I didn't follow through with any of the job offers, as my paradigms and habits would have just followed me. My focus on the job and not on my life would have, more than likely, continued. Long commutes or longer hours would have brought even more of a strain on my family and I would probably have had the same urge to look for and change jobs again, a dynamic that existed my entire career--searching for the next opportunity that would fill a void.

The best decision I have ever made was to focus on my family and myself. Time with my kids was short and I had not been teaching them healthy behavior. The environment within my house was chaotic, and I was the driving force behind it. It wasn't fair to my husband, my kids or to me. I wanted to be healthy. I wanted to be nurturing to my kids. I wanted my kids' memories of their childhood to be painted with color and adventure and fun. But I was not providing my family with the wife and mother I felt they deserved to have.

The decision to give up what I had been using to define myself was made out of a burning desire to be in a positive state and to promote a positive state within my family. This decision was unorthodox as far as how I thought and made decisions at that time. It went against what I had been taught, which was that you don't just quit a job without another to go to. But conventional approaches to a problem will yield conventional results. Sometimes, extraordinary change requires extraordinary decisions.

Once I had time to myself, I started to put into action all that I needed to do in order to go after my desire and dreams, and it translated into my ability to make confident decisions.

I can't identify one specific event or thing I did to make this change. Maybe it was the fact that I was eating breakfast every morning for the first time since high school, a meal that included actual food and not just coffee with lots of creamer. Maybe it was the fact that I was getting more than five hours of sleep per night. I'm sure my changing paradigms and seeing myself through fresh lenses helped. I would see this change in me when I went grocery shopping. I no longer worried about finite details when selecting food off the shelf. I knew what I needed and I reached once for an item, put it in my cart and was off on my way. Although I was not earning a salary and this should have been the time when I exerted a conscious effort to conserve my spending, I was confident that I could make decisions without impacting my budget, so I didn't worry about it. I know it's just grocery shopping that I am talking about, but being able to walk confidently down an aisle, picking out what I needed without having a mental debate with myself was totally symbolic for me! Now I have extra time to check out all the different food and packaging that is something I truly do enjoy, as strange as that may be to some, and I'm okay with that.

Do you have any small decisions that you currently make that take a large amount of time? Why do you think you have a problem making what should be a small decision? Do you have any decisions that you would like to move more effortlessly through? Why?

My grocery store decision-making translated into more challenging aspects of my life as well, like driving what I needed to do to write this book.

As I have increased my networking skills and brought into my life the people who can help me make decisions around things I know nothing about, I have gained confidence. I became an astute follower and intelligent learner, seeking out learning opportunities and people to teach me what they know about getting thoughts to paper, bound in a book, and on shelves. I had to make decisions around how much to spend to finish this book based on no tangible evidence that I would receive a monetary return on my investment. Achieving a dream is priceless but it could not guarantee that it would relieve my family of its financial concerns. I had asked my husband how far we could take this process, as I was sympathetic to the position he was in as the sole income provider. It was my husband's support, my drive to not turn back and comfort in knowing that, if I needed to, I had savings that would allow me to keep moving forward on this dream. Why save the money for retirement when I was living my dream now? If it didn't work out, I had years to re-coup the money. We were making decisions based on no facts, and no guarantees. For a guy who was once leery of the risks associated with a variable mortgage, my husband has come a long way.

How do you make decisions when you don't have all the facts? How does behavior and emotion impact a decision?

I used blind faith to make the most difficult decision at a time when I felt like my personal and professional worlds were out of control. After moving forward and growing as a person with an amazing new confidence in myself, when I look back I don't understand why my decision was so hard. I don't recognize the person I used to see in the mirror, but I do recognize my reflection now. To be honest, I have spent time worrying about the impact of my decision (e.g. paying the mortgage, the impact on the kids when our entertainment budget is tight, worrying about how we are going to pay for sports equipment, paying for bringing this book to life) but I have never regretted my decision as it was made with the right intentions – you can't argue focusing your energies on your family or yourself. Knowing what I know now, and seeing the positive impact of my time with my children, my husband and myself, it just reinforces and validates the decision I made. Being able to re-connect with a childhood dream and write this book makes the decision all that more personal and worth it.

10

Listening to Yourself

"Hey. Over here. No, over the other shoulder. Listen to me."

"No, don't listen to her. Listen to me!"

The comical scenario of good versus evil characters sitting on your shoulders played out in television shows and cartoons is an entertaining and visual method of symbolizing the inner battles and dialogues you can have with yourself when you need to make a decision.

As I said, decision-making is not always an easy thing to do, and making the right decision is sometimes the hardest thing to do. Although making the decision might have been difficult, if it was the right decision, you inherently know it. You still may not feel so great about it in the moment, but you truly believe that your actions are setting off a positive ripple of events.

Your conscious and subconscious minds can do a wonderful job in helping you to make the right decisions among other things, and can guide you in the right direction. But you need to be listening to the inner dialogue within yourself. It's true ... the angel-versus-devil conversations do take place, with the answer to your questions always shining like a beacon. You just have to be aware that it is there to search for.

Your inner dialogue provides a peek into the mental, emotional, spiritual and physical state of your mind and body. Messages are continuously sent to and from your physical and conscious states, communicating the status of the balance of your mind and body. Messages such as breathing heavy after walking one flight of stairs is a gentle reminder that some cardio work incorporated into a daily routine would be a good idea, or a sense that you need to slow down on a stretch of road just before you see the police officer sitting in a speed trap, are examples of ways that your mind is communicating with you on a different level. If you are adept and aware of your environment and surroundings, you will be able to hear its messages. The messages are provided to you, and it is up to you as to whether you will listen to them.

Have you ever made a decision when afterwards that little voice inside your head said "Seriously?" Or you could feel your whole body deflate? Or as the words came out of your mouth, you knew they were wrong but you could not admit that you were scared and were taking the easy road because the harder road was too scary, you felt alone and didn't feel like you have somebody to turn to for help? I have had many situations in my life where that feeling in my gut was completely overwhelming, a beacon shining right in front of me, and I completely ignored it. Sound familiar?

I have learned that listening to yourself can take on many forms: mental, emotional, spiritual and physical. For me, it's connecting with how an emotion makes you feel when it swells up inside you (like the giddy laughter when gazing at your first love perhaps), to using something like a sixth sense to analyze symbols and signs within your environment to guide you in a way you cannot explain, to your body using its prowess to point to an imbalance in your physiological state. The more adept you are at being consciously aware of what is happening around you and to you, the stronger your ability is to keep you motivated, driven and on the right path to achieving your desires.

The body has an amazing ability to send out signals when there is an internal imbalance and things are just not right. These signals can be subtle at first and, if we are attuned to our bodies, we are able to recognize and react to subtle signs. If left alone, these signals can increase and knock pretty loudly. But yet, sometimes we still do not hear them, or we choose to ignore them. From the subconscious level, messages can travel to our conscious mind to attune us to things going on that we cannot always visibly see. Our ability to sense and react to these messages is dependent on our level of ability to acknowledge these messages and in my case, the time to spend to analyze and admit to what my mind and body were telling me.

How to listen to what your body and the environment around you is trying to tell you is not an inherent skill that everyone masters. And being able to pick up on signals from the body or environment is only half the battle as knowing what to do with the signal is equally as important. You can only push your body and mind so far before it is going to tell you, loud and clear, that is has had enough and is tired of being taken advantage of and abused. I had messages from my body years ago that should have been a wake-up call for me to make changes in my life. The messages could not have been any louder, and I chose to ignore them because I created the false belief that there was no immediate impact or concern. I would take care of it "when I had the time."

I have never been overweight even though my diet yo-yoed between okay and not so good with the occasional awesome! I exercised a bit once I had my first child. I didn't drink excessively. I had never smoked. I had low blood pressure and my cholesterol was excellent. However, I had some pretty poor sleeping habits. It took me hours some nights to calm down or ignore the thoughts that would incessantly race through my head. When I did sleep it was not a quality slumber, and I would wake up feeling un-refreshed and with no energy. My alarms going off in the morning (yes alarms; I had an alarm clock with two alarms because I would ignore the first one) would awaken me into a dazed state and I would let out an ominous groan.

Balancing work and life could get petty stressful, especially when both my husband and I worked various shifts. Free time on weekends were typically spent catching up on what could not be done during the week when we were working. One particular weekend, I started my day with a headache forming across the top of my head. No biggie, I remembered thinking. It was just a headache. I took some pain medication that in the past would have relieved me in a reasonable amount of time, but on that day, the headache did not go away. It got worse. Much worse. It grew into the type of headache that exerts pressure around your entire head and just squeezes. Making decisions was impossible as my focus was entirely on the pain. But instead of going home to curl up into the foetal position and nurse my pain, I continued on with my day of completing some house-work and heading out to buy groceries.

Walking into my house carrying bags of groceries, I felt a numbing in my left arm and almost dropped the bag I was carrying. I found the situation odd, but flexed my arm a couple of times and wriggled my fingers to try to rid them of the feeling while continuing on inside. After putting away the groceries I went to check emails but found that I was unable to look at the computer screen without increasing the agonizing pain in my head. I finally admitted I was not able to be productive so I decided to go lie down. I located my husband to let him know what I was doing, but when I tried to speak all I could hear was gibberish. The look on my husband's face was all I needed to confirm that he had also heard the same garbled sounds coming from my mouth. I can remember an immediate feeling of fear running down my spine and I spun on my heel with my husband behind me grabbing the keys and taking me immediately to the hospital with a fear that I couldn't comprehend. Could I be experiencing a stroke?

At the hospital the doctors ran a number of tests and repeated the same questions over and over to me about my symptoms. I was eventually re-leased with an unconfirmed diagnosis but with a number of appointments and follow-ups booked for further testing.

After losing my license to drive for 30 days and undergoing extensive car-diac and neurological testing, the experts concluded that what I had expe-rienced was not a stroke, although they could not confirm the root cause for the symptoms. Tests showed nothing abnormal in my heart or brain. During the 30 days in which I underwent testing I was concerned with the potential long-term health ramifications if I had experienced a stroke. How would it change my diet? Would I need to be medicated for the rest of my life? How could a 30-something without obesity or cholesterol or major health problems have a stroke? The experience should have been a wake-up call for me that the way I was living my life was not jiving with my physiological state.

When the diagnosis came that I had no root cause for my symptoms (I quickly became a virtual doctor and diagnosed myself with having had a severe migraine which can bring on stroke-like symptoms) and there were no further health concerns or recommendations from the experts, my concerns evaporated. The event did not turn into the transformational learning experienced that it could have, and I carried on with what had turned into my self-inflicted pattern of behavior.

I like to think of myself as being an intelligent woman, but my actions following my health scare were idiotic. The few people who knew what happened urged me to slow down and change my lifestyle. But I did not listen. I continued with my paradigm of working hard because I had a good work ethic and that it was just how I was programmed. What I knew but failed to admit was that my work ethic was driving me to increasingly higher stress levels, cracking open a plethora of unpleasant symptoms. And still, I continued to not listen to myself. Over time, cracks grow, longer and deeper. At some point we all have a fault line or a limit as to how much pressure and strain we can put on ourselves. A crack you can seal, a fault you have to heal. Sealing a fault that is deep and profound just covers it up so that you can go on pretending it is not there. It is only a temporary reprieve, not a permanent solution. The seal will eventually fail due to the continuing stress you apply to the fault, causing it to move and shift. In order to fix a fault, you need to go deep into its depths and caverns, and heal it from the bottom all the way to the top. And the reality is that healing can a long time, especially if the root cause is not identified and you continue to treat the symptoms of the crack and not the cause.

Why, as a woman, would I continue on following an obviously destructive path? Have you ever experienced a time when your physical state was sending you messages but you did not listen to them? Why did you ignore them? What happened?

After giving birth to my first child, I suffered from post-partum depression. A trip to the doctor, a diagnosis and a prescription for antidepressants resulted in me feeling better and sealing the crack in my mental well-being, and was part of a cycle I had for how I dealt with my illness, sealing in my feelings and emotions and not healing the cracks.

I didn't realize I suffered from mental illness until my 20s, first as a student then as a mom, mostly because the cultural stigma around mental illness when I was growing up was the elephant in the room that nobody talked about. Admittedly, when I was younger I had no concept of what mental illness even was, other than knowing that some people "acted differently." I was in the dark about a condition that would plague me cyclically in my teen and adult life. I can remember my friends labelling me as being moody, but I just figured it was due to my menstrual cycle.

During the period when I was passive-aggressive with my classmate I experienced anxiety. Fear of having to battle with my classmate in situations I could not avoid resulted in me being unable to focus and suffer heart palpitations. So I went to my doctor and was diagnosed with anxiety. Even at a low dose of anti-depressants, I started to feel better as I was able to exert control over my emotions. During the visit to my doctor, he was supportive of my issues but he spoke with me about the need to gain a better student-life balance. I didn't realize it at the time, but I can now identify that my desire to push through things or work hard, whether it was as a student or career-driven woman, and not listen to the plethora of advice given to me over many years by friends, family, peers, professionals and my leaders had turned into an addiction and that even my doctor's advice and support about protecting my mental health was falling on deaf ears.

I need to thank all the people over the years who were trying to help me, but I had no desire to stop and think about how to think or work differently. I just wanted to start feeling better, to be able to control myself and to get back to working effectively. So if we go back to Chapter 7 when I asked the question "What changed?" what I can add to the story is that the turning-point conversation I had with my classmate came after I had been taking my medication and given myself time to regain clarity and control over myself and my emotions.

With mental health issues on the rise and showing up in media more frequently I know that I am not the first, nor will be the last, woman to feel the pressure of trying to do it all. To juggle all our responsibilities. How do you react to pressure? What techniques do you have to release yourself from stress that could be shared with other women?

In the end, I battled hard to keep myself positive, calm, focused and relaxed. I had a few migraines and sleepless nights were almost guaranteed. My environment was sending me signals that I could no longer ignore and I was impacting my family. My children needed nurturing that I was not able to provide. Signs and messages from every direction in my environment were trumping each other to get acted upon. I did not want to return to my doctor again to confirm a diagnosis that I already knew was for certain. I was prioritizing work commitments over my family commitments trying to help everybody and be the person people needed me to be and the guilt was piling up. Not being able to relax on my 40th birthday and reflecting back on my life and being honest with myself as to what the hell I was doing was my turning point.

As I leapt off the cliff I talked about earlier and continued to soar, I know I will be more than okay because, with my self-intervention, I created a transformational learning experience that re-set my paradigm around work-life balance. That one action of resigning was the first big step I had taken for myself in a long time. With it, I finally convinced myself that I could believe in myself and that I would be okay. That work would continue on without me. That I had created a false-idea that my job defined the person I was. That I could re-define myself however I wanted, reinvent my work-life paradigm and re-connect with my kids and myself. That I could identify success as being my ability to love my husband, my kids and most importantly, myself.

My entire mental state changed once I finished work. My new routine started immediately. I started to receive comments that I looked healthier, smiled more and was more relaxed. I even became more social! My kids really liked their "new Mom." If they were around when people asked if I felt different, they would provide their own insight and feedback that I was no longer so cranky and that I was much more positive. In fact, they would call my behavior out, and if I slipped into a negative state would say things like, "Mom, how can you say that in a positive way?" or point out when I was cranky as it was no longer my typical behavior.

Looking back, I believed that if I worked harder and longer, I could solve all of my problems and get ahead. Could it be that my stress was a result of my own subconscious telling me that I was not physically, emotionally or mentally fulfilled? That my desire to work harder was because there was a force being exerted against me, trying to slow me down? That the universe finally decided I had gained the experience and lessons I needed and put a halt to my path? It was definitely my body's way of sending blatant signals that the situations I was putting myself into and the decisions I was making were not resulting in my happiness and that a serious change was warranted. I had rationalized and convinced myself that I did not need to listen to myself because I was needed, and staying in my current work-life situation was easier than leaving and facing my fears of never being a successful career woman again and failing.

After a few weeks enjoying my new life, I reconnected with my burning desire to help women and girls and to do it through a book, so I started writing. I wasn't sure what my book was going to be about exactly but I spent a lot of time reflecting and thinking about what experiences I had that might be useful to women and girls. Writing became very cathartic for me. It was a positive activity to reflect on the habits and paradigms that led me to that point in my life. As I listened to myself, the ideas for this book and the chapters within it were born. Sometimes my inner voice was so strong and overpowering that I had to pull over in my car and pull out my phone to type down the ideas and thoughts that were streaming through me. Pretty hard to do when it was a constant 20 minutes with two thumbs! My thoughts and visions surrounding this book were completely unpredictable, but when they came, I listened. I have become a much more intelligent listener.

Rate your ability to listen to yourself out of 10, with 10 being intuitively connected to all your dimensions. What are some of the messages from yourself that you have listened to? What are some messages that you have not listened to? What were the results for each? Have you taken any steps to increase your ability to be mindful of messages coming to you? Do you find it easier to listen to certain messages more than others?

Listening to myself set me free and provided me with an opportunity to spend time where it was needed and reflect on what type of life-work balance (not work-life) I wanted. I finally listened to all the people who were genuinely concerned for me over the years and I was quickly able to regain focus and control over my thoughts and emotions.

With my new perspective on life, I made a promise and commitment to myself to become a more attentive student to my environment and to become more aware of my mental, emotional, spiritual and physical states. Leveraging from my powerful coalition of peers and colleagues (shared in Chapter 8), I sought out connections with people who shared my desire for self-improvement and manifesting while empowering others. These connections of women and men helped me to become more in touch with my environment through visualization and meditation so that I had clarity when listening to myself. I now had people I trusted and who could help me recognize what my states were telling me. As I visualized what I wanted this book to be about, and feel how I wanted it to impact women and girls, the words flowed onto the page. Using affirmations and reflecting daily on what I was grateful for played a critical role in me acknowledging how my environments were positively impacting my states. I became much more skilled in understanding how my states impacted my mood and subconscious behaviors, and learned how to control and stop negative feelings or the negativity of others from impacting me. I needed to focus and listen to myself to determine what my needs were so that I could most effectively serve others and myself.

Had I listened to myself all those years ago in that hockey arena and be-lieved that I could go after what I wanted, I might not have journeyed along such a tumultuous path. The outcome to what would have been a different reaction is unknown. But I truly believe that everything happens for a reason and that there is no such thing as coincidence.

My journey has provided me with a number of lessons, tools and experi-ences that were required to write this book and provide stories for others to perhaps learn from. The journey has helped solidify my belief in myself and the lessons I learned have value and purpose to them, and can be used to be a resilient foundation in which to build me up instead of weighing me down. It provided me with the educational background to use critical reflection and storytelling as powerful learning tools for me to share. As unhappy as I once was, my new sense of self continues to amaze me as I continue to go after what I truly desire.

What part of yourself amazes you? How can you use that characteristic to go after what you truly desire? What part of you would you like to develop in order to achieve what you want?

Once I had time to myself, that old feeling of desire trickled back and it was no longer just about me thinking I was going to be a part of some-thing truly amazing. I was part of something amazing. I continue to be giddy and excited about what I'm doing, the challenges I'm overcoming and the breaking through of the barriers I once surrounded myself with. These feelings have grown into what I now know and believe, which is that I am creating something that is amazing and it will continue to grow and be as big as my dreams can envision it.

What would it take to make today the first day of your new journey? What roots have been established and growing in your mind as you reflected on my story and thought about your own dream and desires? What messages has your inner self been sending your way? What would it take for you to begin listening to them?

Plant the seed. Nurture it. Be patient. Establish strong roots, listen to yourself and let your dreams grow.

Maybe I will see you along the way at the crossroads of our paths, as we are all capable of doing things that were once unimaginable when we start to listen to ourselves.

11

You are Perfect

How many times have you heard the phrase "Nobody's perfect?" What was the situation you were in when you heard it? Did you say it? Was it said to you? How did it make you feel?

What is your definition of being perfect right now? Right it down.

I used to believe in that phrase. I had been told that phrase many times. In some situations as I child I believed that I did not have perfect behavior. In fact, I can think of some situations where my behavior was atrocious and I'm sure left my parents embarrassed. As someone who has always wanted to please others, I would try so hard to be the person that somebody needed or wanted me to be so that my behavior was perfect. It was exhausting. Even as an adult leading teams, I wanted to make sure that everybody was happy and their needs met. The larger the team, the harder, more complex, and time-consuming this task was. This resulted in me taking on the burden of time in an attempt to procure positive ratings and views from others, all at the expense of my own mental stress and capacities. And in most cases, it didn't matter. The people I was trying to garner appreciation from did not recognize my efforts and they were the recipients of the same rewards as me, though obtained with much less effort. I let myself feel guilty for not being able to be perfect, and what everybody else needed me to be.

How we perceive perfection is unique to each of us.

As women we may look at other women and admire them for their perfect skin, perfect bodies or seemingly perfect lives. That is what we see on the outside. We rarely get a glimpse of the perfection that exists inside of ourselves, however, because if we can't see it, how do we know it is there, much less believe it's there and that it is perfect? If we have been told for years we are not perfect, how can we start believing something that is the complete opposite of how we see ourselves? Perfection is in our minds. Being able to admit that it is our minds that hold us back on our journey when we talk about having belief or faith in something not tangible that we cannot see. We see the outcomes through our actions and behaviors. But if we listen closely enough to ourselves, we begin to trust ourselves enough to open up our vulnerabilities and see our visions when we close our eyes or allow our minds to wander and daydream.

Your mind is perfect, and your dream and desires are perfect. They are perfect for you and the person that you are. But somewhere along our journey in life we have been bred to believe that life is not perfect and that we are not perfect. Your ability to make mistakes and learn from them is part of your perfection. We need to make mistakes to learn. If we always did everything perfectly we would not learn anything beyond what we were told or read in a book. We wouldn't learn from the reactions or opportunities that imperfect behavior can provide. Mistakes can be gifts. You can open them and see them for what they really are, you can re-gift them hoping that somebody else might have a need for it, or you can leave it unwrapped, never knowing what it inside and if it is something that you really need. Many of our technological and medical advances were due to mistakes that somebody first identified and then capitalized on. If the expert had done everything perfectly, we might not have discovered these miracles.

A score of 10 out of 10 on an athletic performance or math test may mean that we were able to execute the required knowledge or skill at the level required for the competition or test. A perfect score of 10 out of 10 meets the assumption and provides the tangible evidence and proof that yes, perfection was reached. But remember, scores are given based on perceived or assumed notions of perfection. There are many stories of professionals that, even if they were identified as the "best" or "greatest" in their respective careers that they could identify something they would like to change or would try differently in the future in order to challenge themselves and grow and be better. Their thinking is different, as they are seeing the opportunity for growth in what they do, regardless of what others think.

As a parent, I have been guilty of trying to prepare my kids for the reality that life is not perfect and that they are not perfect. It teaches them from an early age how to see themselves and what to believe about themselves. We drag ourselves into a dangerous battle of defining what perfection is and needing to be able to put a label or a picture to it. For whatever reasons, we make perfection seem so far out of logical reach that it is next to impossible to achieve without thinking we need to be a superhero or turning our backs on who we really are. Our job as parents and care givers to children needs to be how figuring out how to best nurture the individual, and support their emotional, mental and spiritual development so that they believe that they are perfect and can do whatever they want to do. We need to start telling ourselves and believing that although our actions and behaviors are not perfect, that we are perfect. And we need to start advocating to our children and youth the same message. There is a difference between who we are and what our actions are and it can have a significant impact on how we see ourselves and how our children feel about themselves and their place in this world.

Perfection is all in our minds and what our perceptions are. What is the perfect house? The perfect job? The perfect car? What you visualize these to be will be different from the visions that I have. And that is okay. What we deem to be perfect can also change as we age and develop different values and beliefs and have different needs based on the stage of life that we are in. For me, the closest thing to a perfect day used to be ticking off all the To Do items on my list (which rarely ever happened),or spending a Friday night cozied up to read with a glass of wine. Now, a perfect day is one where I know I have grown as an individual (which happens every day), helped somebody else to learn or created memories with my kids and hearing "I love you" from them when I tuck them into bed. And it is also curling up on a Friday night reading with a glass of wine.

In short, you are perfect. You need to start believing that. The girl who you are mentoring is perfect. As newborns, they are completely vulnerable to the world. I admit that by telling my children nobody is perfect is meant to shelter them from the hard emotions that come with not meeting a goal or performing their best. As parents, we want to protect our kids and sometimes through nurturing we do more damage than good. It is our job as adults to figure out how to perform our best. Our kids are perfect, and their mistakes and letdowns only add to their perfection if we, as adults, can help them to realize the value in them.

Life is chalk-full of challenges, of opportunities for us to learn about ourselves. They are designed to stretch the limits of our knowledge, will, trust and faith to form a new foundation and a platform from which to leap from and discover the next challenge.

My dream of writing a book is perfect for who I am and it feels right. Writing was always part of me throughout my academic and professions careers in various forms. My journey away from my dream for decades, was not picture-perfect though, and provided me with the opportunities to learn from my mistakes, practice different writing styles, gain the lessons and experiences that I am sharing in this book and meet the people I needed to meet in order to be able to write this book. If I had been perfect, I could probably have written a book about being perfect. And that would have probably been absolutely boring. Mistakes can be exciting! We are human and mistakes help us to grow. They are definitely more entertaining and make for good party conversation if we are willing to poke a little fun at ourselves.

Whatever unique features we each have, they make us who we are. There is nothing wrong with wanting to improve yourself, and to challenge your limits. This is what we are meant to do. We are meant to challenge and create things with our minds and continually grow.

Re-define in your mind what it means to be perfect. What does perfection mean to you now? Write it down. Is it different than what you thought and wrote down at the start of this chapter? If it is different, why?

Perfection is what you make it. You sculpt its meaning. You break down the barriers around it in order to discover it. You own it.

PART III

For Her - The Mentee

12

Desires and Dreams

One of my favorite parts in a popular movie from a few years back is when the main character, a naïve girl who has gained temporary freedom comes into contact with some seemingly unruly characters and asks them about what they want. What their dreams were.

What I like most about dreams is that they do not have any barriers, any biases or play favorites. Everybody has a dream, or many dreams, and the dream does not care who you are, where you live or who your parents are. What is amazing is that you develop your dream for you, nobody else. It is as unique as you are and that is why it is so special.

Everybody has a dream of some sort. The size and difficulty in obtaining the dream can vary from person to person, but it does not minimize the significance of the dream. Some dreams can be simple and easy to accomplish, while other dreams take personal growth and time to complete. The biggest of dreams can take years to grow and develop. Big dreams weave in and out of your life as you acquire the experiences and develop the skills and maturity (and sometimes physical strength!) necessary to steer yourself in the direction and acquire the dream.

To support you through your journey to learn more about yourself and your dreams as you work through this book with your mentor, "Samantha" will share with you in the next chapters in this book, stories about the lessons that she has learned.

Samantha would journal her dreams. As long as she could remember since she was a little girl, she liked writing them down as they helped her make sense of her thoughts. She also liked reading what she had written months ago to see if what she wanted was what she had achieved. Many times, she realized that actions or events that had made her angry or sad when she wrote them down were not as bad as she had thought at the time. How she felt and acted in a situation was relative to what she knew about herself and what she believed at the time. Samantha was able to effortlessly visualize her dreams in her mind, playing out scenarios then translating the dream onto paper. She enjoyed the time she spent fantasizing as she was able to develop a world without boundaries, rules, barriers or people who could stop her from exploring what her imagination could conjure. The written descriptions of her dreams were as vivid as what she could picture in her mind.

Samantha's ability to create fantasies and dreams was a refuge for when she was lonely, troubled or happy, and a pastime she kept hidden from everyone. Some of Samantha's dreams were simple, like writing down her thoughts whenever possible. Some were a little more challenging, like becoming academically stronger in a subject she did not like, which required her to stay focused and spend a whole school year working on. Samantha's dream of what she wanted to be when she grew up...well, that was not always so clear to her as her journaling and visions were not forthcoming, but Samantha knew that if she worked hard in all that she did she would have the knowledge, skills and experience to be ready to pursue her big dream when the time came. She knew that one day she would do something amazing that would change her life and the lives of others, and she was okay knowing that she may have to wait many years for that to happen. She would work on being patient.

Often when Samantha was journaling, her mind would drift off into a world that seemed like a fantasy. When she was younger, she would envision unicorns and rainbows and people dancing and having fun. As she grew older her dreams became more mature and she would see adventures and exotic places, as well as the odd unicorn. Samantha had an ability to make her dreams seem so real, they were like memories she could capture a vivid picture of. A few times, Samantha was caught daydreaming in school by her teachers. It was usually during a class she was not interested in or that she had finished her work in before the rest of the class. Instead of moving onto other work, she would let her mind wander.

"What do I want to be when I grow up?"

Samantha would think about this a lot. In grade school she had big dreams of being an astronaut but had no clue as to what she needed to learn in school to become one. Was studying the stars a prerequisite if you were going to be flying amongst them? Stars did not interest Samantha very much. Okay, so maybe not an astronaut. Samantha would then look at the jobs her parents, aunts and uncles had for a clue as to what her dream job might be. Her Mom did something in an office where she got to wear pretty dresses all the time. Samantha knew that her mother was a "manager" which meant that she was a boss of other people and that she solved problems when things went wrong. Her Mom and Dad would often discuss the "things" over dinner and Samantha had no clue what they were talking about. It was boring stuff.

Samantha's Dad and many of her extended family members were teachers. They all seemed to like their jobs and Samantha could relate to what they were talking about when they all got together, and that's all they could talk about. They would compare their schools, the type of leader their principle was, and the problems they were having with certain students. Samantha admitted these conversations were much more interesting than her Moms were.

Even though Samantha did not know exactly what she wanted to be when she grew up she knew she wanted to help others. To her, helping others was what doctors did. They got to help people every day feel better and be healthy. She didn't like the whole point about having to be around sick people but maybe there was a type of doctor where you didn't have to see people who were sick with colds and the flu. Samantha did not like having either one of those.

The one thing that Samantha wanted to make sure she did in whatever she decided to be when she grew up was to be creative. Her journaling and writing were an escape for her and something she really enjoyed. Maybe she could combine her desire to write with a dream of being a doctor and write medical books. Hmmm. Not a bad idea but she would have to wait to learn all the information about what needed to go into a medical book.

The problem with wanting to go after something she saw in a dream was that Samantha did not have the knowledge to do what she was doing in her dream. To be a doctor, well, that needed many years of school so what could Samantha do to start learning now so that when she learned stuff in school it would be easier? Samantha did not have anybody she could talk to about doctor stuff since she did not know any doctors (other than her own) and her parents were not science people so they could not help her. Who could help her and point her in the direction of where to get knowledge? That question stumped Samantha as much as the question about what she wanted to be when she grew up. How would she know who to look for when she had questions?

Samantha decided that maybe she would start with small dreams where she could see results sooner than later. Small dreams were less scary and if Samantha needed to learn things on her own, it didn't seem too hard. Besides, going after a bunch of the small dreams she was thinking about in her mind might make room for new, slightly bigger, medium-sized dreams for her to see. As she achieved her medium-sized dreams then maybe one day there would be enough room for her to see exactly what her dream job would be.

If anything, this would fill the time between now and when she got moving on her big dream of doing something extraordinary in her life when she grew up. All that she did know with her years of wisdom as a grade-school girl was that she wanted to help people.

She knew that life would help her to figure that out.

Reflection Questions:

1) Do you have a dream? Can you write it down? If you can't think of one that is okay. As you read through the chapters with your mentor and you get a dream, write it down.

2) When do you feel yourself daydreaming? What do you like about daydreaming?

3) What makes you passionate or happy with your dream?

4) How can you express your dreams to other people?

5) Do you have small or big dreams or both?

6) Who can you share your dream with?

7) What are things that you can do to go after your dream now? What needs to wait for the future? What do you need in order to go after your dream?

13

Believing in Yourself

Sometimes new situations are thrown your way that you have no say in. Somebody else has made a decision for you, but in most cases (like if it was your parents or caregiver who made the choice for you), the decision was made with love and the desire for you to learn about yourself and grow. Although you may not always agree with what your parents, teacher or mentor want to get you involved in or what new experiences they want to expose you to, be open and accept it for what it is: something to challenge you that you would never have done if it had been left up to you. You might learn a lot about yourself that surprises you. Accept the challenge and perform your best.

To go back to Samantha, her parents changed the school that she went to at the end of her primary school year. They had made the decision without her and Samantha just had to go along with it. She didn't know anybody else at the new school or if she would like it, as it wasn't a "normal" school. It was a school for kids that had an interest in the arts, specifically singing and playing instruments. Samantha didn't understand why her parents decided to move her to this school. When Samantha learned that she would have to read sheet music, play a stringed instrument, sing and become an actress she felt uncomfortable and scared, believing there was no way she could do all that. What were her parents thinking? She was a soccer player, not a singer. Was this their way of being cruel? What had she done that was so wrong she was being punished this way?

On the first day at her new school, both of Samantha's parents dropped her off. They came with her into the school to help locate her new classroom and meet her new teacher, Mrs. Wilkinson. Mrs. Wilkinson smiled at Samantha and welcomed her to the class, then showed Samantha where her locker and desk were. Samantha's desk was at the very back of the classroom. "Perfect," Samantha thought, as all she wanted to do was hide in the back and just watch everybody else. She was nervous and still not sure if this was the right thing for her parents to do.

On the back of the chair directly in front of Samantha's desk was a nametag that read Abrianna. Samantha thought that it was a really pretty name and very unique. She had never heard of that name before, assumed it was a girl's name, and wondered what the girl looked like. It was not long before Abrianna flowed gracefully into the classroom with a smile on her face. Samantha was amazed at how it looked like she glided into the room. She herself had trudged into the class with her head hung low. How could somebody be so happy to start a new school and not know anybody?

Mrs. Wilkinson greeted Abrianna and her Dad and gave them the same routine of showing them where the lockers and desk were. As Abrianna approached her desk, Samantha could see that she was looking at her with a smile.

"You don't seem like the type of person who will kick the back of my chair," Abrianna said to Samantha with a laugh as she pulled the orange chair out from under the desk, letting it scrape on the floor.

Samantha immediately thought that Abrianna was funny and laughed.

"Only if I see you falling asleep," Samantha chided back to her new friend.

"Good one! You're funny. My name is Abrianna Glyn. I'm from Oakwood Public in the north end of the city. What's your name?" Abrianna asked this as she unpacked some books and writing tools from her backpack and placed them into her desk.

"I'm Samantha Jackson. I went to Scottsdale Public. I'm the only one here from my school. Did you come by yourself?" Samantha was feeling completely vulnerable with the person she did not know.

"Nope. There are about five of us in this class that are from Oakwood. Somebody from this school came to Oakwood last year and did a big presentation on why the school is so awesome, so a bunch of us asked our parents to sign us up."

Abrianna was excited and bubbly, as she had finished unpacking her things and now sat in her chair pay full attention to Samantha.

"I can introduce you to everybody at recess if you want and you can hang out with us. We are pretty much an outgoing bunch," Abrianna offered this looking at Samantha sympathetically.

"I'd like that, thank you," Samantha replied then turned her attention to Mrs. Wilkinson who was starting the class.

At recess, Abrianna was true to her word and introduced Samantha to all of her friends from Oakwood Public: Ryan Peters, Damon Edwards, Claire McKnight and Juliette Matthews. Samantha was surprised to learn that they all had interest in the arts, either because they already played at least one instrument or they danced or did stage performance. Although everyone was really nice and included Samantha in their conversations, she really felt out of place.

After recess Mrs. Wilkinson led the class to the music room where their conductor, Mr. Rusk, was waiting for them behind a collection of more stringed instruments than Samantha could count. Wow! Samantha could not believe the school had so many instruments. She was amazed at how beautiful the wood was. Many were so shiny you could see your reflection.

"Mr. Rusk, what if we have never played an instrument before? How are we going to learn?" a curly blond-haired asked. Samantha was relieved that somebody had read her mind and asked the question.

Good question. How many of you in this class have never played an instrument before?" Mr. Rusk looked across the class of students and started to count the number of hands that were raised. "Eight, nine, 10, 12, 14. Okay. So out of a class of 20, 14 of you have never played a musical instrument before."

Mr. Rusk must have seen the scared looks on the faces of most of the students in the class because he then shared softly, "Music is like any other creative art, and you can use it to express yourself. Whether you already play an instrument does not matter. We are all going to start at the same level. If you dance, you already know how to feel and respond to rhythm. If you play another instrument like the piano then reading sheet music will be a little more natural for you. If you write or draw, instead of holding a pen or pencil, your bow now becomes an extension of your arm."

Samantha enjoyed how Mr. Rusk explained this. As she liked to do creative writing, she could relate to his piece about the bow being a substitute for her pen. Hearing the connection between whatever musical instrument she chose and her writing made her relax but she still had only a wavering belief that she could pull this music stuff off.

Samantha listened intently as Mr. Rusk explained each of the different instruments that they would choose from. He also played some different classical music songs and described how each type of instrument could be picked out from the overall melody.

Samantha thought about her available choices. Their grade was only allowed to pick between a violin and a viola. The violin was the instrument that she could easily pick out in all of the songs. The viola seemed to fade into the background and you didn't seem to notice it there, but if it were missing you would hear the difference.

When Samantha was asked for her choice, she chose the viola--a supporting instrument that hid in the background, just like what Samantha wanted to do.

Once all the class had made their choice and they were sized for their instruments, Mrs. Wilkinson returned and brought the class to the vocal room. It was here that the class would be singing. Samantha was already exhausted from music class and longed for lunch to arrive so she could re-fuel her brain. At least in vocal class, there were seats and the class sat down as the vocal teacher, Mrs. Onado, introduced herself.

"Singing is just about using your voice to communicate. You already talk to communicate so singing is like putting more variety in the tones that you use when talking. You are telling a story and singing changes the tune of the story and adds emotion so that you can sometimes feel the energy of the story," Mrs. Onado shared this with the class in a sweet voice that sounded like it was designed to sing.

Samantha felt connected when Mrs. Onado also connected music to telling a story. It relieved Samantha of some stress but this was short-lived as Mrs. Onado instructed the class to line up across the front of the class so that they could each sing a scale. First, Samantha had no idea what that meant, and second you mean they had to sing by themselves in front of the whole class?

Samantha started to sweat and she could feel her heart beating. She had sung before but usually in her own room and the volume of the radio would have just drowned out her voice so that nobody would have heard her anyway. What if she was a terrible singer?

Mrs. Onado played and sang what Samantha learned was a scale. She was happy that the students at the other end of the line were chosen to start singing first. As each student sang their scale, Samantha could pick out many other students who showed obvious signs of being nervous. Their voices quivered or cracked and some faces were red. By the time the line got to Samantha she figured she had nothing to lose.

She stepped forward and sang her scale. When she was done, she stepped back into line and stared at the floor.

"Samantha, have you sung before?" Mrs. Onado asked.

"Um, no. I just sing in my room to the radio," Samantha replied.

"Really? Your voice sounds like it is trained. Well, then, you are a soprano," said Mrs. Onado.

Samantha did not know what a soprano was and became frustrated with all the new words and terminology she was learning on her first day. How was she supposed to do well if she didn't even understand the language that all the teachers were speaking? Samantha felt like she would never catch up in knowing what this school was about. She didn't believe she belonged at the school. Her parents had made a big mistake.

The rest of the day went along without any more surprises or music talk. Samantha was relieved to be able to just listen to Mrs. Wilkinson take them through a math lesson. Math Samantha "got." Everything else she was exposed to that day, she didn't get.

When Samantha returned home that night after school, her parents were excited to hear about how her first day went. Samantha didn't know how to describe to them that they day was awful, that she was completely out of place and that she still couldn't believe that her parents had made the right decision.

"I didn't like it," Samantha started. "Why did you send me there? I don't play a musical instrument. I can't read sheet music. I chose to play the viola and their sheet music is even stranger looking than the violins! All the music teachers speak a foreign language. They were good about linking music with other creative outlets but I don't believe I can learn all of this new stuff."

Samantha's parents were quiet for a moment and looked at each other from across the table.

"Samantha," her Mom started, "We made the decision to send you to that school because you have a musical gift."

Samantha had no idea what her mom was talking about. What gift? She couldn't even call herself a piano player and she only sang in the privacy of her own room.

"Your voice is beautiful. It is completely on pitch with whatever song you sing. You can sing high and you can sing pretty low. But whatever note you sing, it is perfect. You sing perfectly and your Dad and I want to you have to experience to discover and grow that talent," Samantha's mom finished gently.

Samantha was embarrassed. All this time she thought nobody could hear her sing! Her parents heard all along and they never said a word.

"Why didn't you tell me you could hear me sing?" Samantha asked.

"Well, honey, for the longest time we didn't realize it was you. We thought it was the music since you turn it up so loud," Samantha's Dad explained. "Then one day we realized that the songs were changing but the voice singing the songs was not changing. It was you and you sounded beautiful."

"Like a rock star!" Samantha's Mom added in looking proud.

"I never realized that. So you really think I can sing? Good enough to be in a choir?" Samantha was starting to see her singing in a different light. Because she had never sung with others before she had never compared her talent to anyone else and had just figured her singing was nothing special. She was starting to believe that maybe her parents had made a good decision, and that she could do well.

"Of course! We would never set you up to fail! Your Dad and I think that you can take on the challenge. You are artistic with your writing and singing, so we are just having you extend that creativity into string music and drama. You will be wonderful and you will soar not fall," Samantha's Mom got up from her chair to give Samantha a warm hug.

Samantha thought about what her parents said for the rest of the night and the next day before school. If her parents were so confident in her singing and ability to apply that to other forms of expression, then maybe she could believe that she could do it too.

Samantha walked into her classroom that second day in a different mood. She was confident and walked in proud, not flowing in like Abrianna, but not trudging in like she had done yesterday. She smiled at Abrianna and said good morning to her as she sat down in her chair. Samantha looked at her class schedule to see that she had music class first thing in the morning.

Samantha went into music class with a better attitude. She was trying to stay positive about playing an instrument she knew nothing about. Once the set up her chin rest and prepped her bow, she was ready. Mr. Rusk took the class through finger placement and then a scale. Samantha felt a rush of pride as she knew what a scale was. She would close her eyes and visualize where her fingers were to be placed as she moved her bow back and forth to force out the scale. Samantha imagined that the bow was her pencil and she was moving it creating sound instead of creating a work. It felt comfortable and Samantha was starting to feel more positive about her ability to perform.

At the end of the day after a great lunch with her new friends who all shared their fears about holding and playing the instruments, vocal class was up next. Samantha walked into the classroom and people's names were written on colored pieces of paper, sitting on the blue chairs. Samantha found her name on a pink paper that said "soprano." Samantha had searched the term last night on the Internet and learned that sopranos were able to sing in the upper range of notes. The really high ones.

Mrs. Onado took the class through a couple of scales, which Samantha belted out proudly, then explained the differences in the voices in the classrooms. She then handed out music books for the class to work from. The first song they were going to learn was the national anthem, but instead of everybody singing it in the same tune, they were going to learn the alternate melodies to the song. As the class each learned how to sing their separate parts Mrs. Onado asked that they put all the parts together. When they finished, Samantha felt a tingling excitement throughout her body. She felt that the class sounded beautiful and could feel the energy and vibration of all of them singing together.

Samantha finished off her second day on a high note. She had conquered her fear of the viola, connected with her passion for singing and started to envision herself succeeding in her new school. She started to believe in herself and that she could take on this challenge. She believed that her parents made the right decision.

Reflection Questions:
1) Why did Samantha not believe in herself?
2) What barriers and walls did Samantha put up around her because she did not believe in herself?
3) Do you believe that there is something that you can't do? If so, what can you do to change your belief?
4) What can happen if you believe that you can't do something?
5) What do you believe that you do really well? Why?
6) If you could do anything you wanted, what do you want to do?

14

Sticking to It – You CAN Do It!

Dreams do not typically come true overnight. The idea of the dream takes time to grow in your mind, and sometimes it is hard to visualize what the dream is supposed to be or mean. Movies make it look like dreams can be attained in an hour and a half. This is not typically the case but the lessons that the movie is trying to teach are valuable: that it is good for you to believe in yourself, to have a dream and to go after it as it can bring you happiness along with a lot of other positive feelings, including helping you believe in yourself. The time you need to realize your dream is as unique as you. It cannot be measured and planned out. Even once you realize what your dream is, the "how" behind what needs to be done in order to achieve the dream is not always obvious and may be a complete mystery. Going after a dream can take time and if so, it will require you to stick to believing in the dream, no matter how much time it takes. Sticking to what you believe in is a powerful behavior and the reward when you get what you want is that much more special.

In Samantha's mind, her soccer skills were pretty good. She started playing soccer when the lack-luster experience of playing softball was not meeting her physical or mental needs. Samantha knew that she enjoyed running and watched the boys at school play soccer in the yard at recess. Some of the girls played soccer with the boys and were pretty good. Not knowing anything about the game, she asked her parents to change sports, and they agreed.

Samantha attended practices in the beginning because she knew that she had a lot to learn. Not just the rules of the game, but what position she preferred to play and what position she absolutely did not want to play (goalie). Learning positions taught Samantha a lot about herself; was she a driver who wanted to score the goals as a forward, or was she more of a protector on defence? Samantha liked playing forward. It was easy for her to count the number of goals or assists that she got in a game and she could write down her results for each game to see improvement. After playing soccer for a couple of years she was able to see how much she had improved since starting.

After playing soccer for only a couple of years, Samantha entertained a dream to play at a competitive level.

Girls in her schoolyard had talked about trying out for a team that travelled to different cities. Travelling seemed really exciting to Samantha, and she had always thought the "soccer girls" were really nice and wanted to have something more in common with them. So Samantha mustered up the courage to ask her parents if she could try out for the city team. And they said "no". They reminded Samantha that she had only a few years of experience playing soccer and that girls trying out for the city team had been playing soccer for many years.

"Maybe in a few years, when you have more experience," her parents told her.

Samantha was crushed. She had wanted to try out so badly and her parents did not seem to understand that. Watching the girls in the schoolyard, Samantha did not think they were more skilled than she was. So tryouts took place and the girls from school made the team. They played in cities all around during the summer and Samantha was reluctant to even play in her recreational level. It wasn't fair that her parents hadn't even let her tryout.

In the fall, school started up again and Samantha saw the girls from the city team playing soccer in the field again. Samantha had to admit, their skills seemed to have really improved over the summer. They were able to do really neat tricks hitting the ball off of various body parts that Samantha realized she could not do. Maybe her parents were right, maybe she did not have enough experience.

One day at the end of recess, Samantha asked one of soccer girls, Deidra, where she had learned the ball tricks.

"On my competitive team. Doing the tricks actually helps us learn how to control the ball in a game situation," Deidra smiled, and Samantha came up with the courage to then ask, "Can you show me next recess how to do that?"

"Sure. You should join us some time. The boys let us have extra girls on the field because they think that they are better than us," Deidra laughed and then ran into the school before they were late.

Samantha thought about Deidra's words, and it became clear. Samantha had been watching the soccer girls play but had never actually asked to play. Deep down, Samantha had been scared to play because she might not have been as good as they were and did not want to be embarrassed. If she wasn't good enough, then her parents would have been right that she did not have enough experience.

The next day, Samantha brought her soccer shoes to school and asked Deidra to show her the fancy tricks at the start of recess. Samantha could not believe how hard it was to bounce the ball in the air from foot to foot. She spent more time chasing the ball as it rolled away from her than kicking it with her feet. Deidra made it look effortless! After trying the tricks, Samantha joined the soccer girls on the field to play against the boys. She was huffing and puffing within a few minutes as she was not used to the fast-pace. Samantha soon realized that maybe her parents were right and she was not ready for competitive soccer. But she really wanted to play competitively, especially since Deidra was becoming a good friend.

So Samantha made the decision that the best way for her to learn how to be a better soccer was not by watching, but by playing with soccer players better than her. She no longer watched soccer being played at recess; she joined in the games. She knew that in order to still meet her dream of playing competitively she needed to get better and that it would take time and hard work.

Samantha spent the spring and early summer working hard on passing, shooting and ball control during practices so that in a game she would not have to think about what her feet were doing. After one of her games, Samantha's parents greeted her along with a woman that looked really young that she did not recognize. Her parents introduced the young woman as Coach Carrie, a local university student who was putting together a "select" competitive team made up of girls from the recreational teams around the city to travel at the end of the summer to different soccer tournaments. Coach Carrie was wondering if Samantha was interested in being on the team.

Samantha was ecstatic and close to tears! Somebody had sought her out to be on a competitive team that she did not have to try out for! The coach explained that he had been watching her skills develop over the early part of the season and saw a huge improvement and wanted to give her a challenge. Samantha could not believe that her dream to play at a competitive level was coming true, and felt proud that she had made the commitment to practice and try her hardest at improving her skills to make her a better player.

Samantha played soccer at the "select" level for a total of two summers. Because the "select" team involved additional playing time on top of her recreational league, she was playing soccer up to four times a week. Samantha learned that this was the same amount of soccer that the city team played. Deidra helped Samantha during the summer with her skills and Samantha was able to measure that she was getting more goals each summer.

After her second year at the "select" level, Samantha asked her parents if she could try out for the city team. This time they said "yes". At tryouts, Samantha was not nervous, as she was confident in her skills that she had been working on over the past few summers. As cuts were made and the number of players left in tryouts got smaller, Samantha's confidence in herself grew.

Samantha learned that you could reach your dream with persistence and belief in yourself. She learned that the paths to achieving a dream have a funny way of showing up when you are focusing your energy on attaining the dream, and when you are not expecting it. A valuable lesson was that if you have a dream that you are really excited about, you have to be persistent in going after it as it will not happen overnight. It requires continual hard work and finding different opportunities to reach your dream.

Reflection Questions:
1) What does persistence mean to you?
2) What are the different ways you can stick to what you need to do to achieve your goal?
3) How can others help you with your persistence?
4) Have you ever been persistent in going after something? What actions did you take to be persistent in achieving what you wanted? What would you do differently?
5) What lessons did you learn by being persistent?
6) Why is persistence important when you are going after your dream?

15

Learning From Others

As dreams are unique to each person, opinions and experiences that each of us have are also unique and present opportunities to share with others. We can all learn from each other. Learning from others can be obvious like sitting in a classroom and listening to presentations by teachers or your fellow students, but learning can also be done by interacting with friends and through your involvement in different activities. When you are trying something new or interacting with others, you are learning--you probably just don't realize it.

For Samantha, soon after starting a new year in school, she walked into her classroom one day and immediately noticed something different. As she entered the classroom, Samantha noticed that the desks had been moved from rows to groups of six and that there was a girl she did not recognize sitting in one of the groups of tables. The girl looked at Samantha. Samantha smiled and began to scour the desks and found that hers was beside where the girl was sitting.

"Hi. I'm Samantha," Samantha smiled as she put her books down on top of her desk and pulled out her chair.

The girl smiled back at Samantha, not saying anything and moved her gaze to the floor. Samantha noticed that the girl was dressed in a different style that she had not seen before. She had on a white top with a multi-colored scarf around her neck and her hair up in a bun. She looked very grown up and much fancier than Samantha who was wearing jean shorts and a striped tank top. Samantha put her books away and then chatted with her classmates as they started to drift into the room and begin the hunt for their desks. Soon, the bell rang and Samantha's teacher, Mrs. Knowles, walked into the classroom. After the announcements were finished, she walked over to the desk where the new girl was sitting, who was looking really nervous.

"Good morning, everyone. First, I am sure you have noticed that the desks have been moved around. I have arranged the desks into groups to create a different learning environment so that you can learn together as a small community of learners on top of learning as part of a whole class. We also have a new student in our class. Her name is Mirabelle and she moved here from France with her family. She does not speak much English but I am sure that everyone will help her to learn quickly but please be patient with her. I'm sure she will have no problems teaching you all a couple of French words. Please welcome Mirabelle to our classroom."

There was a chorus of "Hi, Mirabelle" from the class followed by laughter as the class found it humorous that they had spoken in unison but had an array of versions on how to say Mirabelle's name. Some of the students waved and Samantha turned to look at her classmate.

"France? That's awesome! I haven't travelled far away from this city let alone travelled across the world. Let me know if there is an English word that you don't know. I can help," Samantha whispered as class begun.

"Merci. Thank you," Mirabelle whispered back looking relieved that the introductions were over. Samantha thought that Mirabelle's accent was beautiful.

When it was time for recess, Samantha looked at Mirabelle and said, "Come with me. I will introduce to you my friends." In the school yard Samantha introduced the new student to her friends who were all curious about her, about France and about how to say bad words in French. Mirabelle looked to be more relaxed than she had in the classroom even though she mostly listened to what the girls were saying and did not join in the conversation.

At the end of the day, Samantha walked out of the school with Mirabelle and asked if she had enjoyed her first day at school.

"Oui. Yes," Mirabelle replied. "The school is different than back in France but people are very nice. Thank you for being nice."

From day one, Samantha and Mirabelle became fast friends. Samantha realized that she really enjoyed learning from Mirabelle. Samantha's school was made up of pretty much the same type of kids and there was not a lot of variety in culture. She didn't know of any other kids in the school that had even come from a different city let alone a different country! Mirabelle had different thoughts and opinions on any subject they talked about and Samantha enjoyed hearing Mirabelle's perspective. Samantha realized that because Murielle had really different experiences from growing up in a different country that she did things differently and behaved differently. Mirabelle would share with Samantha that her interest in art came from her ability to visit all the different museums that were in Paris and that she did not like going to the beach in her new country as the water was way too cold compared to the warm Mediterranean Sea in the south of France.

What Samantha learned most from Mirabelle was that people were as unique as dreams. That it is okay to not think the same as everybody else as different opinions lead to discussions instead of everybody just agreeing so that no conversation ensues. Samantha learned that it could be boring when everybody had the same opinion. Samantha was fascinated to learn about how Mirabelle celebrated things like birthdays and holidays and loved going over to her house for dinner as her Dad was a chef and cooked really different food. Samantha never ate hamburgers and hot dogs at Mirabelle's house. Although Samantha was fascinated by her new friend and enjoyed learning from her, Samantha soon learned that not everybody was friendly or comfortable with people who are different.

One day at recess Samantha, Mirabelle and some other girls were having a discussion about a new app that was becoming very popular on social media for making up groups so that they could chat on-line. The group discussed asking each of their parents to buy the app and then they would create a group made up of just themselves so that they could chat when at home. When Mirabelle shared her opinion though, the conversation no longer became funny.

"I am not able to buy apps like this one as my parents won't allow me. A family friend had a bad experience with the wrong information being shared on social media. People would get really mean, even friends," Mirabelle shared with the group.

"Why do you always have to have a different opinion? Why can't you just agree with us? Having to have discussions all the time because you don't agree with us is getting to be so boring and a waste of time. I don't care about your difference of opinion." Mirabelle looked shocked as Whitney blasted out these mean thoughts of Mirabelle in front of the group.

"I'm sorry, excuse-moi. I don't have the same experiences as you but I wanted to share what experiences I do have. I guess I have not lived here long enough to have the same opinions as you do," Mirabelle apologized, looking sorry. Samantha was confused about why Murielle was even apologizing, as she didn't feel that Mirabelle had said anything wrong and she liked that Mirabelle had different experiences.

For the rest of the day, Mirabelle did not say anything. This was not typical for her, as she had shared with Samantha that she participated in class because it was a way for her to practice her English. Plus she had felt that the class seemed interested in her difference of opinion and her stories.

"I love learning from you. You don't think and feel and do the same as we do and I think that is what makes you special. You make things less boring and I find you fascinating," Samantha shared with her friend on their way home after school. She felt bad for her but did not know what to say.

Samantha was quiet during dinner that evening and her mother noticed. "What's wrong? Did something happen at school today?" Samantha's mother asked when they were clearing the table after dinner.

"Somebody said something really mean to Mirabelle today. They said that they don't care about her opinion and that she should be thinking like us since she lives here now," Samantha shared.

"And what do you think?" asked her mother.

"I think that it is wrong to not listen to Mirabelle's opinion. I love learning from her as she has neat ideas that are different from mine. Sometimes her way of doing things is better than mine! And sometimes she likes how I do things more than how she learned to do it. I think that we all can be right but together we can be great! Why doesn't everyone feel this way?" Samantha asked.

Samantha's mother was quiet for a moment as she thought of how to explain social change and justice to her daughter.

"We all grow up learning values and beliefs from our parents and the culture, city and country that we live in. We grow up not thinking that there is any different way to do something or think. For example, how did you learn to like eating broccoli? Did you have a choice?" shared Samantha's mother.

Samantha shook her head. "I don't know how I started to like broccoli. I just do."

"We as parents fed you broccoli as a baby because that is what we like to eat--so we gave it to you to eat. You did not necessarily have a choice to learn if you liked it or not. You just did because we influenced that as parents. The same thing happens with how we think and do things. We influence you. TV programs that you and your friends watch can influence you to believe that you really need us to buy you something. What you learn is not the only way to do something. It is just the one way that you know how to do something."

"By you being friends with Mirabelle, you get to learn from her about how other people in the world live and think. It is not right or wrong. It is different. Being open to learning from others can expose a whole new world of learning for you. It can make you appreciate what you do have and know, and sometimes you can learn easier or better ways to do things, or help you learn something new that you like but would have never known if you didn't take a chance to learn from others." Samantha's mother was getting excited as she talked about Samantha being fortunate enough to have the opportunity to learn different things.

"Just like you don't like that the kids at school are judging Mirabelle, you should not judge them. Our world is changing and we are beginning to share more of our cultures with each other as people become more open to moving around the world to work or be with family. It creates new opportunities for people to learn from each other, but we need to respect others if they do not take the opportunities to learn from others," Samantha's mother cautioned her, in a soft voice. She looked at Samantha to see if she understood what was being said to her. Samantha understood and she knew how to help her friend.

The next day, Mirabelle came late and did not hang out with the groups of girls before school. She hurried into the classroom as soon as she could after the bell rang and went straight to her desk where she sat quietly, her head looking down.

"Good morning, Mirabelle. Are you okay?" Samantha asked her friend.

"Bonjour, Samantha. No, I am not okay. I am still sad from what Whitney said to me yesterday. I don't know what I said wrong," Mirabelle whispered softly, her voice cracking as she tried not to cry.

"I talked with my Mom about this last night. I learned something from her and I think it can help you," Samantha tried to maneuver her head underneath Mirabelle's so that she could see Mirabelle's face but it was not working. Samantha started talking anyway, hoping that her friend would at least listen to her.

"Whenever I eat at your house we always eat French cooking right?" Samantha started. Mirabelle's head did not move. Samantha continued.

"You told me that you don't eat hamburgers and hot dogs as you and your family have a desire to keep cooking and eating the way you did back home. So without even trying a hamburger or hot dog, you have made an opinion about it. You are not wrong in your thinking. It's just your beliefs and your family's beliefs. It's the same with Whitney. With the app, she perceives that your way of thinking is not right. That is her belief. You both are allowed to have your own opinions because that is part of who you are. The difference between the two of you is that you are being respectful of other people's beliefs. Whitney was rude in not being respectful of your opinion. Whitney may not change her mind on what she thinks of that app any more than you many change your mind about hot dogs."

Samantha watched as Mirabelle lifted her head and looked at Samantha. Her eyes were wide.

"I never thought of it that way. It is true. I do think and act differently than you all do. I like some of the things that you do better than how I do them, but then there are still things that I like better that are from how I learned growing up." Mirabelle smiled. "I like that you taught me that. It makes me feel better. I always like learning from you. You challenge me to think differently and you have interesting stories. They are very different from my stories."

"Your stories make things around here a lot more interesting. I can't imagine you not being here. I am glad to have you as my friend as I have only started to learn from you. I want to learn a lot more."

Reflection Questions:

1) What have you learned from somebody else (not including your parent or teacher)? How did you learn the new activity or knowledge?

2) Do you know if you have taught somebody else something? How do you know?

3) Do you think that you can learn from all the different types of people around you?

4) Why do you think that not everybody wants to learn from others?

5) What could you do to help people learn from you, and for you to learn from others?

6) How does learning from others play a role in you going after your dream?

16

Surrounding Yourself With the Best

Everybody is constantly changing. As you learn new things in school, through your parents and coaches, mentors or friends, you can either accept the message that is being communicated to you or reject it. If you accept it, it can impact how you think, and importantly, how you behave.

Samantha loved the scene in one of her favorite movies when the main character, a strong-willed girl battling her own barriers, shared her opinion to a group of strangers, not caring who was around to hear. The result was that the characters was able to excite the crowd to stand behind her and help her get what she wanted. It was one of Samantha's favorite parts in the movie because the scene reinforced that there is absolutely nothing wrong with having a dream, and that it proves that when one person gets excited and shares an idea or their dream that their excitement is contagious and makes others happy and want to share their dreams too and help others to pursue theirs! The supporting characters in the movie all learned something about themselves and each other as they rallied to support the main character in achieving her dream. People who do not judge you and are willing to learn about you and support you when you need it are those that you can call your friends.

Samantha had a large group of friends that she had known since her first days in school. They had literally grown up with each other and there were not many changes in her social circle with new friends coming in and old friends going out. This consistency helped Samantha to feel secure in knowing that whenever she went out for recess that she had a large group of friends to choose from to play with.

A new school year had started, and would be the last for Samantha and her friends in grade school, and Samantha was excited to see many of her friends that she had not seen over the summer. Samantha had been in many different summer camps where she surprised herself and met some really neat new friends, including one from Europe! It was not like Samantha to be outgoing and introduce herself to strangers but since she did not have friends in all of her camps, she was forced to get to know at least one new person in each camp so that she had somebody to play with for the week.

Samantha met up with some of her friends before the start of school to try and catch up on all the summer activities before everyone separated into their new classes for the morning. She was happy to hear that her friends missed her as much as she missed them and that they agreed that they should have called or seen each other more during the summer break because so much happened from growing a couple of inches, to bodies changing, to being more interested in boys and not so interested in the "kiddie stuff" anymore. Samantha was amazed at how much can change in a couple of months. Samantha even realized that she had changed over the summer; she definitely grew a couple of inches and her mother complained that she had outgrown her shoes again and that her shorts were a little too short. This was fine with Samantha as it meant that a shopping trip to a big mall in a neighboring city to buy back-to-school outfits was needed! Samantha liked the back-to-school shopping as it meant that she could spend time with just her Mom having "girl time" and her Mom would let Samantha be a little independent, making some of her own decisions on what outfits and clothes to buy.

At first recess, Samantha met up with her friends by the soccer field. As everyone was wearing a new back-to-school outfit, nobody wanted to ruin it by playing soccer. So the girls gathered around to continue catching up from the summer. During the conversations, Samantha noticed that a few of the girls, Natalia and Linda, talked the most and did not let others speak for long without interrupting them. Samantha also noticed that Natalia and Linda would say to the other girls that what they had done over the summer was "immature." In fact, they did not have many nice things to say to the others girls at all! Natalia and Linda did have a pretty cool summer going together with their Moms to New York City and they looked like they had studied magazines on how to dress and do their hair fancy as Samantha felt that they looked older and more mature than the rest of the girls. Their adventures in New York City seemed so much more fascinating than summer camp. They had gorgeous hairstyles and cool clothes from their summer and all Samantha had was some fun memories that nobody else could see.

Sometimes after school, Samantha would walk with Mirabelle to her house and hang out until her parents picked her up on the way home from work. Nights when she did not go to Mirabelle's she made an agreement with her parents that she would walk directly home then call one of her parents when she arrived. As she was leaving the school grounds by herself on her way home, Samantha met up with Natalia and Linda who were hanging out at the back of the school with some boys she recognized who used to go to their school but who had graduated. Samantha asked the girls if they wanted to all walk home together since Natalia and Linda lived just a few blocks from Samantha's house.

"No thanks, we are going to hang out around here for a bit. Do you want to stay with us?" asked Natalia glancing at Samantha quickly before returning her gaze to the boy she was standing next to.

"Uh, I'd like to but I can't. I have to go home and call my parents to let them know I got home OK. If I'm late they will worry," Samantha was torn. Her parents had just awarded her with some independence and were letting her walk home by herself and stay at home by herself for a short time before they got home. Samantha did not want to break her promise to her parents, especially on the first day!

"Seriously? You can't stay for five minutes? How will your parents know?" Linda chirped while wrinkling her nose.

Samantha was getting uncomfortable and looked down at the ground. She debated with herself. Her parents knew Natalia and Linda, and it was only five minutes and Linda was right, how would her parents know if she hung around for five minutes? She wanted to hang out with the girls but did not want to break her parents' rules, especially on the first day!

"Uh, ok. Five minutes," Samantha gave in.

"Awesome! This is Sean and Carter," Natalia said as she pointed to the two boys.

Samantha hung out with Natalia and Linda and the boys, but did not say much. She quickly felt out of place as there were three girls and only two boys and Natalia and Linda were extremely focused on keeping the attention from the boys on them. They were also talking about things that Samantha was not comfortable with. After what felt like five minutes, Samantha spoke up.

"I think I'm going to head home. I'll see you guys tomorrow," Samantha commented looking at Natalia and Linda. When Samantha got no reaction or even a glance from the girls to know that they had even heard her, she walked away.

When she got home, Samantha saw that there was a message on the phone. As she put down her bag she played the messaged and gasped when she heard her Dad's voice and it was angry. Samantha quickly looked at the clock and her heart started to race as she realized it was 45 minutes after school had finished. Samantha felt her skin go cold and she got nervous. It was the first day with her new independence and she had blown it! Her parents were not going to be happy, and based on her Dad's message it was a pretty accurate thought.

Samantha's fingers were shaking as she picked up the phone and dialed her Dad's cell phone number. A good excuse or possible story went flying through her head as to what she would tell her Dad to justify why she was late. As the phone rang Samantha could not think of a story that would be believable. She could not bring herself to blatantly lie to her Dad.

"Hello?" Samantha's Dad's voice was calm, but did not have the typical upbeat sound. Samantha knew she was in trouble as he was using the voice that she knew he used when he was really trying to control his emotions.

"Hi, Dad." Samantha said, not saying anything more.

"Did you forget to do something or are you just getting home now?" Samantha's Dad asked, in the same calm, cool voice.

"Uh, I ran into Natalia and Linda after school and we were catching up on summer stuff and I lost track of time," Samantha informed her Dad, cringing slightly as she knew it was a stretch of the truth.

"What was the arrangement that we agreed upon?"

"That I would come home directly after school and call you," Samantha recited the words that she had promised over and over to her parents during her attempts over the summer to let them trust her to walk home by herself.

"Well, we will have to talk about this when your Mom and I get home tonight. I'll be home by five o'clock."

"Okay. I can set the table for dinner," Samantha offered, hoping the gesture would help keep her in her parents' good books and take attention off of the fact that she had not kept her end of the arrangement.

Samantha had the table set and was reading on the couch when her parents arrived home and came inside the house after chatting on the driveway for a bit (Samantha had been watching out the front window). Her parents were calm but over dinner expressed their disappointment in Samantha for not sticking to the agreement. They agreed that, with it being the first day, there was a lot to catch up on with friends so they were going to overlook the lateness that day.

Samantha was relieved. She did not want to go to a babysitter after school. So after school the next day, she was focused on walking straight home. As Samantha was leaving school property, she saw Natalia and Linda wave at her to come over.

Samantha walked over to the girls.

"Hi guys, what's up?"

"We are just hanging around. Want to join us again?" Linda asked not even glancing up from what she was looking at on her phone.

"Thanks, but I need to get home. I got in trouble yesterday for being late."

"Are you serious? You were 10 minutes late, and you got in trouble? Boy, your parents are strict and are treating you like a baby. I remember they used to have all those rules when we would come over and play. Too many rules ruin the fun," Natalia exclaimed, laughing.

Samantha continued down the path to the end of the schoolyard. All the way she could hear Natalia and Linda laughing and calling other girls in the yard over. Samantha missed spending time with Natalia and Linda as they had been friends for years but she did not want to let her parents down again. If she did, she might not have any freedom to walk home by herself. On the other hand, Samantha did not want to spend too much time with the girls as they were focused on different things that Samantha was okay not knowing or talking about. The two girls had seemed to magically mature over the summer and grown a large vocabulary and index on what Samantha thought were adult subjects.

Over the next few months, Natalia and Linda began to accumulate a large following of girls, like an entourage. Girls who were awestruck by their fancy clothes and hairstyles, the most up-to-date phones and seemingly endless knowledge of pop culture and social media trends. They acted like they were the leaders of the girls who all started to dress and talk the same way as them. Samantha started to avoid walking home in the direction that would cause her to walk by the group, as they would sometimes call her out.

It all started innocently, but Samantha did not like it.

"You'd better hurry up and get home to your parents and get your bottle ready!" Natalia would yell at her as Samantha walked by.

"I give her a "six"! She at least she tried to style her hair!" Trina bellowed one day.

"No, a "five"! Look at those shoes!" Linda commented.

The verbal insults became very personal to Samantha when the girls started to "grade" or "rank" her on her style and looks.

Samantha began to hate walking home at the end of school. She thought of taking a different route but that would take longer and she did not want to get in trouble with her parents for taking too long to get home, but she did not want to tell them about what was going on. Samantha was beginning to believe what the girls were saying about her. That she was a baby, and that she was ugly. Samantha began to be uncomfortable with who she was and how she looked.

One day in gym class, Samantha was playing basketball. She was working hard and getting baskets for her team who cheered her on. Her team was beating the team that Natalia and Linda were on, and they did not like it. They did not want their styled hair to get sweaty so they were not putting in a lot of effort, but they also did not like getting beaten.

In the second half, the teacher was called out of the gym to speak with another teacher. Samantha was dribbling the ball down the court when she heard, "What a ball hog. You'd think that her team might want a chance to score."

The voice belonged to Natalia. With the teacher still out of the gym, other girls on Natalia's team began to make comments.

"Who needs a team when Samantha thinks she can do it all?" cried Heather.

"I didn't know there was an "I" in the word team!" chattered Melanie.

"Show off!" Linda yelled.

Samantha stopped running with the ball and stood there stunned. Why were the girls being mean to her? Her team was cheering for her as they were winning and happy, right? Samantha began to doubt that her team was actually rooting for her. She dropped the ball and went and sat at the end of the bench by herself, fighting back tears.

The game continued on and the teacher returned just before the bell rang. The girls all ran out of the gym to change and get ready for lunch. Everyone but Samantha. She did not want to be in a change room with the girls, fearful of the teasing and other put-downs that would be hurled at her.

Samantha was so focused on not crying that she did not realize that somebody had approached her.

"Are you okay?" Deidra asked.

The concern from her friend was more than what Samantha could handle. Tears began to stream down Samantha's face. Deidra and Abrianna looked at each other and sat down on either side of Samantha and put their arms around Samantha's shoulders.

"They were pretty mean to you. I'm sorry for not sticking up for you but I was scared," Abrianna said softly.

"I don't know what has happened to Natalia and Linda. They have become really mean this year. I'm glad we have not been hanging around with them. I'm sorry for not sticking up for you too," Deidra shared.

Samantha shook her head and wiped the tears from her face. "Thank you," was all that she could mutter in between sniffles. "I'm glad you two are here now. I didn't know what to do. I didn't mean to be a ball hog!" Samantha shared and started to cry again.

"You were not being a ball hog! The team was cheering you on because you were doing so awesome! We were excited for you. You were totally controlling the game, which is probably what Natalia and Linda didn't like. The attention was not on them," Deidra said.

"I don't know what I did wrong for them to hate me this year. I tried being friends but I can't stay late after school with them and I get uncomfortable when they talk about clothes and boys as I'm not into that stuff, but they make me feel horrible about myself," Samantha shared with her friends for the first time.

"We know. That's why we have not been hanging out with them this year, but a lot of the other girls think they are cool and just want to copy what they are doing," Abrianna commented.

Deidra shook her head. "No, they are copying them because they are afraid of them. They are just going along with them because it's the easier thing to do. Do you think that Melanie or Heather would have made those comments if Natalia and Linda were not there? No way! We used to be best friends with them, and once they saw that you were upset you could tell that they felt bad about what they said. The difference is that Natalia and Linda seemed to be happier once they saw how upset you were."

"I don't know what to do. They tease me when I walk home from school, and I can't walk home any other way or else I will be late and I don't want my parents to find out. I feel bad enough and am embarrassed," Samantha sighed.

"First of all, do not be embarrassed for who you are. You are beautiful and unique and a kind person. Why, you could have hurled insults back at them but you didn't. You are classier than that. You are smarter than that. You need to believe that. Don't believe them," Deidra supported her friend, "And I don't want them being mean to you. So if they are mean to you, they will have to deal with me!"

"Me too," Abrianna chimed in, smiling and holding her palm in the air that Deidra slapped and the girls giggled. "Girl power!" the two of them cheered.

"We will walk you out of the school yard tonight. We'll see what Natalia and Linda say about that," Deidra started to plan where they would meet after school to walk Samantha out of the yard.

Samantha felt better with the support of her friends, knowing that they truly wanted to help her. She got up from the bench, ready to continue on with her day, but feeling queasy about what the end of the day would bring. The only thing that made her feel better was knowing that she had friends supporting her.

At the end of school the bell rang and Samantha proceeded to her locker, the pre-determined meeting place with Deidra and Abrianna. Once the three of them were ready to go, they walked out of the school together. Putting on a brave face, Samantha walked outside and immediately located Natalia and Linda at the end of the schoolyard. Right where Samantha needed to go.

As Samantha, Deidra and Abrianna approached the group of girls, they could hear Natalia call out, "Look. She had to bring reinforcements! Look who really does need babysitters," Natalia and Linda laughed while the other girls in the group chuckled weakly, looking uncomfortable.

Samantha, Deidra and Abrianna ignored the comments and the group and continued on their way off the school grounds. The lack of response seemed to anger Natalia and Linda.

"What? Are you too good to talk to us now? We aren't friends anymore?" Linda scoffed before calling Samantha a derogatory name.

At that point Samantha stopped walking. Anger was brewing inside of her. The derogatory name had pushed Samantha too far. It was one thing for the girls to tease her, but to call her a name while being culturally insensitive to others did not sit with Samantha. Samantha made the decision to stand up for herself, and to also stand up to the people innocently dragged into a conversation by someone who was ignorant of what she was saying.

"Linda, you are right. We aren't friends anymore. Friends would not tease and talk badly to each other. Friends would not be mean to each other. Friends support each other when they are doing well. These are all things that you and Natalia are not doing. So by definition, you are not my friend." Samantha was not yelling at Linda but talking very confidently as at that moment, she believed in herself and who she was, which was a kind, supportive and caring person. A person that she had started to believe was of no value. Linda putting down somebody else who was not there to stand up for themselves fueled Samantha to make the decision to stand up for those who were unable to stand up for themselves and to show Linda that she was not going to take the bullying anymore. It was a risky decision, but for the sake of her own self-belief and for the culture that Linda had cursed, Samantha made the decision that it was a risk worth taking.

"Do you know the definition of the word that you just called me?" Samantha challenged Linda.

Linda, looking startled, shook her head. "It's just a word. Relax," Linda roller her eyes and gave a weak laugh looking at Natalia for support who looked uncomfortable as she kept her gaze locked onto whatever was on her phone.

Linda's dismissive behavior made Samantha angrier. "It is not just a word. Using that word without knowing its meaning makes you ignorant. You were being insensitive to others by using that word. How would you feel if I called you something?"

Samantha quickly stopped herself. Although she was angry she did not want to hurt Linda like she and Natalia had hurt her. She did not want to be the kind of person that Linda and Natalia had turned into. She wanted to remain true to the person she was, so she made the decision to stop what she was saying and be that person.

"I'm sorry we aren't friends anymore, but I don't want friends who are mean to each other and to others. I want friends like Deidra and Abrianna who are here to support me and make sure I am okay, even if it means going against what is the popular thing to do. I want friends who will hold me up and support me when I need to be courageous, not hide behind a phone. Sometimes the right decisions are hard decisions, but I made the right decision to not be friends with you this year," Samantha said calmly, with a hint of sadness in her voice because of the lost friendships she once valued not too long ago.

Samantha, Deidra and Abrianna continued to the end of the schoolyard without another word uttered by Natalia, Linda or any of the other girls. Samantha did not bother to look back once because she did not care what was happening behind her. She was feeling empowered and proud of herself for making the decision to stand up for herself and others. She was happy she decided to share her troubles with her two caring friends who were walking on each side of her, chatting happily to keep the mood light.

The next day at school, Melanie and Heather approached Samantha while she was playing soccer with Deidra and Abrianna.

"We're sorry for bullying you in gym class the other day," Melanie started, looking and sounding apologetic. "We were going along with Natalia and Linda as they had been bugging us earlier in the game so it was a relief for their attention to be on somebody else."

"It doesn't make what we did any better though," Heather chimed in. "We're sorry. After you said what you did last night, some of us told Natalia and Linda that they were being bullies and that we didn't want to hang around people like that. So we also decided to leave. Thank you for deciding to stand up to them. They were not expecting it and you made us think about what it really meant to be a friend. And Natalia and Linda were not being our friends. Deidra and Abrianna helped us to realize that friends stick up for each other, even when it can be scary and hard." Heather and Melanie exchanged glances and smiles.

"Thank you for apologizing," Samantha said with a warm smile. "I appreciate the fact that it must have been hard for you to do that."

"Thanks. So do you have room for two more to play?" Melanie asked with a sheepish smile, looking down at the soccer ball perched underneath Samantha's foot.

"We were strategizing about how to beat the boys during the game at lunch. And the more minds the better the ideas we can come up with," Samantha smiled as she and Deidra led the group in a collaborative discussion on how to win the next game.

Reflection Questions:

1) Why does having the "best" people impact your ability to achieve your dream?
2) How do you feel when people say negative things to you? How does that change your mood?
3) Have you had to make the decision to distance yourself from a friend who was not being nice to you? Why?
4) Explain how your friends support you when you need them.
5) How do you support your friends when they need you?
6) What role should your friends play when you go after what you really want?

17

Making Decisions

Decision-making is a skill that you learn as you make choices. If your parents make all the decisions for you, then you do not learn how to practice and exercise your ability to think your actions through, or debate with yourself the pros and cons of the decision. You need to learn from your successes and learn even more from your mistakes. You need to learn how to weigh out the risks of what you are going to do versus not doing something or finding an alternative solution.

Whatever your decision is, you need to be comfortable with it as you are the one who, ultimately, is responsible for and has accountability for the decision. You need to be able to be comfortable with your actions. If you reflect on your behavior, you will answer to yourself and your subconscious will tell you if you made the right decision, if you are willing to listen to yourself.

Samantha lived next door to Aiden who was the same age as her. They had always lived beside each other since they were infants so they grew up knowing about each other and playing with each other. Aiden also liked to play soccer so he and Samantha would regularly kick the ball around when Savannah was not around or sometimes the three of them would play together. For fun, they would practice kicking and heading the ball over the fence that separated their yards. Once Samantha had started to play soccer at recess in grade school she would play against Aiden and have a fun time trying to maneuver around him and keep the ball away from him. Once they graduated into high school and lost their recesses, their gym classes were separated based on gender so there were not many opportunities for Samantha and Aiden to participate in friendly competition against each other. So when a friendly battle could be waged over the fence, Samantha was all in and leading the way! Her confidence in her soccer skills since being selected to play on the city competitive teams had grown to where she did not see her games against Aiden to be about who was better, boy or girl, but was about using their evenly matched skills to challenge and improve the other.

Samantha enjoyed being friends with a boy as she felt that boys had different views from girls, and they stayed away from the drama that girls tended to create through what seemed like endless competition with each other. Samantha believed that the girls were really in competition with each other and drew other girls into conflict in order to avoid having to admit that they themselves were the source of the conflict. With boys, Samantha felt that they were more relaxed with themselves and dealt with their aggression more efficiently (but not so effectively sometimes as fists could be involved). Having a boy as a friend was refreshing and up to that point, straightforward and uncomplicated.

Samantha noticed one day while she and Aiden were partaking in their usual skill development of kicking the soccer ball over the fence that Aiden was unusually quiet. Normally she and Aiden could easily carry on a conversation about any topic while they were practicing. Their conversation only interrupted by laughter and encouragement when one of them made a rookie error or made an amazing move that the other could only faintly see through the cracks between the fence boards. Not thinking anything was wrong or different, Samantha initiated conversation with Aiden.

"Are you okay? You seem awfully quiet today," Samantha asked in her best nonchalant manner as she kicked the ball over the fence.

Aiden did not immediately answer her. He was looking down at the red and white ball that he had trapped under his foot from her kick and was rolling it around on the grass.

"I'm fine. Just thinking about stuff," Aiden replied sheepishly.

"Oh. Is it school? Have you selected your courses for next year yet? I'm having trouble deciding on which science classes to take and if I have room for an extra English writing course. Sometimes there is too much choice and I do not want to go to summer school just to take extra classes." Samantha scrunched up her nose at the idea of going to summer school just to take a class for fun. If she were to go to summer school it would be to upgrade a class she already took in order to bring up her marks so they were the best possible for when she applied to whatever post-secondary school and program she decided on.

"No, it has nothing to do with school," Aiden sighed, still looking down at the ground but no longer circling the ball around with his foot. Instead he was now grabbing onto the bottom of his shirt and playing with it. Samantha watched Aiden and thought that he looked like he was ready to be sick.

"Do you want to go inside? You don't look too good. Maybe you are getting sick," Samantha offered to her friend who was acting very peculiarly and she was getting concerned.

"No. Can you come closer to the fence? I want to ask you something," Aiden blurted out quickly, really fidgeting with his shirt now.

"Sure. What's up? You're not going to throw up on me are you?" Samantha tried to use humor to lighten the mood that had gotten pretty heavy from her perspective.

"Um, so you know how we've been friends for a really long time and we get along really well. Well … I was wondering if you would like to be my girlfriend?" Aiden sped through his speech that Samantha figured he had probably practiced a ton.

Samantha did not answer. She was trying to digest what had just happened. Did Aiden just ask her out? Was her mind playing tricks on her? Did she hear it right? No couldn't be. She and Aiden were just friends.

"I'm sorry. Did you ask me to be your girlfriend?" Samantha asked to verify that she had heard correctly, moving her head so that she could get a better view of him through the fence. Since she couldn't she hopped up on the fence board and looked over and saw that Aiden's face was red and he was sweaty. At that moment, Samantha knew that Aiden was serious about the question he had asked her.

"Yes," was all that Aiden could muster, standing completely still.

Aiden's question made Samantha think differently about her friend. She had never thought of Aiden in that way. They were friends. She was not really that interested in boys like some of the girls were at the end of grade school and moving into high school, Samantha noticed that a lot more girls were becoming interested in boys but she didn't see them any differently.

Samantha did not know what to do or how to respond but she felt bad for her friend who had just used all his courage to ask one question and she felt that her friend deserved an answer, except that she was not sure what that answer should be. So she came up with a decision that she felt was a compromise and she felt good about.

"Thank you for asking. You must have been nervous. I've never had a boyfriend before so I don't know much about what to do or if I will be a good girlfriend but I am willing to try. So, yes, I will be your girlfriend," Samantha replied to Aiden. His face had started to beam when the word "yes" came out of Samantha's mouth.

Over the next few weeks Samantha tried to figure out how to transition from being Aiden's friend to his girlfriend. She watched how her friends' interacted with their boyfriends and tried to mimic some of the flirty laughs they had, and giving him a peck on the cheek. Aiden would beam at her when she did this and Samantha would smile back but pull back from him in anticipation of a potential lip lock. She could not figure out a way to make herself comfortable as a girlfriend and she started to think that there was something wrong with her.

Samantha felt that she had become lost as a person by being part of a couple – she was no longer an individual unit. It was always "Aiden& Samantha" or "Samantha and Aiden" and there was an assumption that Samantha's activities were to include Aiden. Samantha was not comfortable with no longer having her own identity. She wanted people to know her for who she was, not know her as being 50 per cent of a couple.

One day, Aiden grabbed her hand at her locker. Samantha was a little shocked. It felt strange to hold his hand. They used to hold hands when playing ring-around-the-rosy or Bulldog but that felt so different than holding his hand now. She had never realized before how strong it was. Samantha had never thought of Aiden before as anything more than a friend so to look at him differently was unsettling. When she tried to change her mind on how she visualized Aiden, as a boyfriend and not just a friend, she had a hard time. She missed the innocent games of soccer over the fence. They had pretty much stopped those since they declared their commitment to each other. Now they just hung out, talking. And now they were holding hands. Samantha was yearning for the days where they were competing against each other, not holding each other. As the days went by, Samantha began to get more uncomfortable being a girlfriend, especially being Aiden's girlfriend. She wanted her friend back. She wanted her identity back.

Samantha knew that she needed to make a decision about what was right for her. She needed to talk through her emotions with somebody as was getting anxious and it was causing tension between her and Aiden and she did not feel that was fair to her friend.

One morning while crunching away on her cereal, Samantha decided to ask her Mom for advice.

"Mom, can I ask you a question?" Samantha said quietly, not even looking up at her Mom.

Samantha's Mom sensed that this was going to be a serious conversation and that her daughter was looking for support so she sat down at the table, opposite to Samantha.

Gently, she said, "Sure you can. What's on your mind?"

Samantha did not know where to begin. She was so confused that she started to cry and had trouble catching her breath. Samantha's Mom immediately came over to her side of the table and hugged her and stroked her hair, waiting patiently until Samantha calmed down.

With a deep breath, Samantha started, "You know how Aiden and I are together?"

"Yes."

"Well, I can't seem to find a way to be comfortable with the whole thing. I like Aiden as a friend and we have a fun time together, but now, being his girlfriend it's different and not in a good way."

Samantha noticed that her mom seemed to relax a little bit once she provided some information on the decision that she needed to make. It's like she had been preparing herself to have a different kind of conversation. Samantha couldn't figure out what that could have been.

"Honey, you need to first be honest with yourself and make a decision as to what you want. Do you want to have Aiden as a boyfriend or just as a friend? You need to decide what it is you need in a relationship and if Aiden can give that to you. Just realize that he may not want to be friends right away if you break up. How you decide to have the conversation and the words that you decide to use will impact how he is going to react to the situation."

"But what would you do?"

"I'm sorry honey, but I can't make that decision for you. Only you can.

Just know that you have to make a decision that you feel is right for you and you are comfortable with. Then you need to decide how you are going to tell Aiden. He deserves to be treated respectfully and needs to know if you do not feel the same way he does. There is nothing wrong with that, we all mature and are ready for relationships at different times, but you need to make that decision. The sooner, the better out of respect for Aiden." Samantha's mom coached her.

Samantha had been hoping that her mom would tell her what to do. When she was younger she used to do that all the time. And now, when she wanted to be told what to do she couldn't get it. Samantha didn't understand all of her parents' decisions right away, but usually after time she would figure out what their intention had been. After all, she was in high school and getting to the point where she should be able to make decision on her own, especially when it came to if she was ready to date or not.

Samantha thought about her dilemma that night. To help her visualize the problem and maybe identify a solution, she wrote out on a paper what she liked about being Aiden's girlfriend and what she did not like. To no surprise, her "did not like" list was much longer. Samantha knew the decision that she needed to make and she knew that Aiden would not be happy. She knew that by continuing on with the charade of being his girlfriend it would only make it harder to break up with him later on. Samantha was not ready to be anybody's girlfriend. She made the decision to be her own person, not a couple.

The next day on the walk to school, Aiden went to grab Samantha's hand and she pulled it away.

"What's wrong?" Aiden asked, stopping and looking at her.

Samantha could feel the tears welling up in her eyes immediately. She did not want to hurt Aiden but she needed to be honest and truthful with herself.

Samantha took a deep breath to help hold back the tears, then started, "Aiden, I have always enjoyed our friendship, but I can't be your girlfriend. As must as I like you as a friend, I am not ready to be in a relationship. I am comfortable around you, but I am not comfortable being your girlfriend. I'm sorry, but I need to be honest and committed to myself first before I can be the best person that I can be for somebody else."

Samantha waited. She watched Aiden's face as it was expressionless but she could see in his eyes that he was thinking. "Okay, wow, that was not what I was expecting," he said slowly. Samantha felt horrible but knew that it was the right decision to make.

"I need some time to myself. I'll still walk you to school but I don't think we should hang out at all today. Will you be okay walking home from school?" Aiden asked. Samantha's heart was breaking. Even after what she had just done, Aiden was still concerned for her safety.

"I'll be fine, thanks," Samantha replied and the both faced forward and walked to school in silence. When they got to school they parted ways toward their lockers without saying a word.

Samantha's friend honed in immediately when they saw her that something was wrong, so she told them. There were shocked gasps but they understood that if Samantha was not ready for a relationship you could not rush it, force it or fake it. It would not be healthy for either person.

After school Samantha walked home by herself and since it was a nice day, decided to relax by the pool to do her homework. Maybe the extra sun would help to life her spirits. Soon after opening her books, Samantha felt water splash onto her legs. She looked up and sure enough, they were wet. She looked into the pool and saw the source of her shower. A black and white soccer ball.

Samantha put her book down on the deck and turned off her music. She glanced at her fence and could faintly see a figure between the boards. It was Aiden. A warm feeling, not from the sun, came over her and Samantha ran into the house to put her shoes on. She then returned to the pool to fish out the soccer ball and proceeded to kick it over the fence.

She had her friend back.

Reflection Questions:
1) What was the hard decision that Samantha had to make?
2) Why is it difficult to make decisions even when you know it is the right thing to do?
3) What are some consequences of not making a decision that feels right to you?
4) How do you feel when you have had to make a hard decision that was also a right decision? How did you come up with the decision? What skills did you learn in order to make the decision?
5) What did you learn about yourself when you have had to make a hard decision?
6) What decisions do you need to make related to your dream?

18

Listening to Yourself

Making decisions can be a complex process. The range of difficulty that comes with decision-making is huge; from easy decisions where you don't have to think to difficult decisions where you need to obtain feedback and learn knowledge from others in order to arm yourself with the right information to make the best decision for you. Many people will try and persuade your decision-making or offer advice. Although the advice and recommendations you get from listening to others may sound good, remember it is all based on what information you have told them and their perception of the problem based on their own knowledge and experience, beliefs and values. The only person who can make the best decision for you is you.

Samantha loved high school. She enjoyed the challenges that it offered academically and she had met many amazing and supportive people who she was glad to call her friends. Although some days came with their challenges, Samantha saw each challenge as a problem that she wanted to solve, and believed that she could solve any problem.

Getting a good mark in calculus, algebra and geometry was a challenge that Samantha was glad she took on and conquered. Samantha had spent years since Grade 1 saying that she was not strong in mathematics. As most university programs required advanced classes in mathematics, Samantha knew that she would have to take math classes throughout high school until the very end. As Samantha did not want a poor mark in her math classes to bring down her grade point average and affect her potential to get into the university she wanted, she knew that she had to overcome her self-belief that she was a poor math student in order to get the best marks.

The drive to keep up her marks, not only in her math classes but also in every class that she took, resulted in Samantha having a GPA of 4.0. Her outside activities in soccer, her part-time jobs babysitting and as a camp counselor, and extracurricular work on the school yearbook committee and writing clubs made Samantha a well-rounded student at least that is what Samantha's mother would always tell her.

Samantha needed to make a decision. She had really good examples of when she had to make big decision throughout high school that helped to validate her self-belief and the values that she had in herself. The decision she had to make this time though was about taking all that she had learned into what would be her adult life. Samantha needed to decide on not only what universities to apply to but what programs she wanted to study.

Samantha loved both English and Biology and took as many classes as she could in high school to learn as much as she could in each subject. English allowed Samantha to use her creative side, to write stories and poetry. Samantha loved standing up in front of the class giving presentations and sharing what she had learned. Sometimes her English projects would not follow the status quo of what others in her class were writing about but Samantha was okay with that. Thinking and writing about topics that she was passionate about made the project not even seem like doing work. It was fun and when the project was written and presented Samantha would be extremely proud of herself. Samantha even won a couple of writing and literary awards that she proudly displayed in a cabinet in her room.

Biology, however, allowed Samantha to use her analytical thinking mind. Biology satisfied Samantha's curiosity about how things were made and to discover on a daily basis the amazing universe and what humans could do. Samantha was really good at recalling data and labelling charts and diagrams from memory. Her favorite component of her last biology class was the unit on dissection. To be able to see the organs and systems and how they were integrated, not just in her mind but in front of her on the lab bench, was fascinating.

The problem was that being really good at two very different subjects made it tricky to know which one to study in university. Testing that Samantha had completed with her high school guidance counselor indicated that she would be good at gardening and careers related to nature.

Seriously? Samantha was not able to come up with one job she wanted where she would work outdoors. She was not able to see past a one-dimensional view of jobs in nature – her literal mind took the careers suggested to be literally, in nature. No thanks.

Samantha shared her dilemma with her friend Deidra who was unable to relate.

"That's a great problem to have," Deidra would say, "I'm passionate about history so to me it's obvious that I will apply to do an arts degree with a focus on history. You are lucky that you have options."

But Samantha did not see the possession of options as being lucky. Samantha saw it as a barrier and a sign that she was not focused enough, or being honest enough with herself.

Secretly, Samantha loved nurturing her creative side. In her spare time she would write short stories and poetry. Writing was a great outlet for her when she was upset or angry. Why, being angry was a great catalyst for coming up with poems as she was emotionally connected to the content of the poems! Writing was sometimes like therapy for Samantha, a way to put her thoughts onto paper and then re-read them to see if they made sense. Writing provided a world of fantasy where she would not judge herself and where her creativity was endless. Samantha did not spend her spare time with her nose in medical textbooks memorizing nitrogen cycles or analyzing human anatomy, although reading up on microbiology and their impact in food manufacturing was pretty interesting.

When Samantha talked to her parents about what program to study in university, the sciences were the only focus of conversation. So Samantha's parents only talked to her about what area of science to focus on and then what universities had good science programs. Molecular biology? Biochemistry? Biotechnology? Although the areas of specialization were plentiful, there was no specific area that held more interest for Samantha. The options either had a bit of what she was curious about or were topics that she had not even heard of! That encouraged Samantha as it meant that there were a lot of different jobs that would need a science degree.

When Samantha did think about pursuing a degree where she could write, she did not know where to start. She did not know anybody else who liked to write. Most of her friends were applying to science programs or specific arts programs like history or political science. Nobody was applying to complete an English degree and Samantha had no idea what you could even do with an English degree. Samantha did not have the confidence to ask her guidance counselor what other options were available around writing. Samantha was careful to think of potential job opportunities as she did not want to spend money on a degree and at the end not have a job. With lots of science options, it must mean that there were lots of science jobs. Right?

So Samantha completed her applications. She applied to multiple universities for their science programs. As she was completing the applications, Samantha had to write articles about herself and her achievements in order to be considered for scholarships. Samantha spent a lot of time writing and polishing her works, and enjoyed doing it. Again, she did not consider it to be work and actually found it to be the most fun part of the application process. As she wrote about herself, Samantha would experience emotions that she could not put a name to. It wasn't sadness but it definitely was not happiness. It was not frustration but certainly was not excitement. Samantha could not remember having this feeling before and she was confused over it. What she was doing did not feel wrong but it also did not feel right. It did not make any sense to Samantha. She had done everything right in high school: got high grades, played sports, had great friends, worked on different committees. So why did filling out applications for a program that she liked and excelled in make her feel the way she felt?

The desire to write and be creative on her applications was pulling on Samantha. Re-writing the applications and supporting documentation did not seem to rid her of the nagging feeling that she had. So without putting much thought into it and, knowing that the application deadline was approaching, Samantha decided to fill out a single application for an English program at the local university. Filing out the application felt effortless to Samantha as the words she chose to describe herself and what she had done in her life flowed effortlessly from her. A feeling of serenity and power came over her as she completed the application, and she felt that the words were not just flowing out of her, they were flowing through her, to truly connect with the unknown person who would be reading her application, holding her future in their grasp.

After completing her application for the English program, Samantha sent it off and felt entirely at ease. The unknown feeling that had been ravaging Samantha for weeks dissipated without Samantha even realizing it. Not knowing what it meant, Samantha proceeded to do what most high school seniors were doing at that time, which was to wait.

The weeks went by after the university application date passed. Samantha postulated that what program she was meant to enrol in would be unveiled through whatever acceptance letters she received. Soon, the large packages were arriving at her door congratulating her on her acceptance and scholarships to the different universities that she had applied to for their science programs. Samantha's parents were ecstatic, especially around the topic of scholarships! They submitted to Samantha their requests as to what program to accept based on the scholarship amount. Samantha was excited and relieved to be receiving acceptance packages as it meant that she would at least have options as to where and what she was going to study. What Samantha was not relieved about was that unknown feeling had returned and was plaguing her mind constantly throughout the day, becoming almost an obsession for her mind. Samantha found it hard to concentrate on much else and she was starting to feel ill not knowing the response to her English application.

Samantha started to get honest with herself and really think about what this was trying to say to her. She decided to write out the thoughts that were running through her mind in an attempt to calm it down and rid it of the clamoring nuisance that was making her anxious. Samantha sat down with pen and paper, relaxed and just let her thoughts go. She wrote down whatever words popped into her head, drew sometimes, and wrote down multiple thoughts, feelings, emotions and activities that made her feel good about herself. At the end, Samantha sat back and looked at what was on her paper. What stared back at her seemed like a cryptic message at first, but once Samantha looked at what was written as a whole and not as individual words, a picture began to form in her mind. Samantha became a little emotional when she realized that what was bothering her was her creative self needing to be heard and accepted, and asking for her to take a risk and to choose creative thought over analytical thought. Once Samantha realized what her creative self was trying to tell her, she started to listen to herself to help her make a decision on her university career.

When the acceptance letter to the English program arrived in the mail, Samantha was overjoyed. She pranced around the house like a giddy schoolgirl, laughter bubbling up inside of her in uncontrollable waves. She took a risk on listening to herself and it was working out, the evidence right in her hands. Samantha knew the decision that she needed to make, and that she needed to listen to herself, and only herself, in order to make it. She knew that by following what she felt and thought was so right would be the right decision. Although it was not the logical decision based on her known career options, was not what her parents thought she should do, was not going to be anything her friends were studying, she wanted to follow the burning desire she was feeling and accept the offer to the English program.

Samantha listened to herself as she made the really big decision that would be the start of her new journey into adulthood and into discovering herself and what she really could do. She did not know what a future job or career could be with her English degree but following her burning desire and listening to herself offered her all the help and guidance she would need to navigate her new path and course-correct her if needed to keep her in line with discovering a dream career.

Samantha was going after her dream.

Reflection Questions:
1) What could have happened to Samantha if she did not listen to herself?
2) What are some signs that you have felt when listening to yourself? Did you listen? Why or why not? What were the results?
3) Why do you think it took so long for Samantha to listen to herself? What would you say to her if she were sitting next to you?
4) What actions did Samantha take that were right? Why?
5) Why is it important to listen to yourself?
6) What do you think the purpose is for listening to yourself? How does this relate to your dream?
7) How does listening to yourself impact decisions that you need to make?
8) Have you listened to yourself and gone after something you had a burning desire for?

19

You Are Perfect

The day was beautiful, a little windy but sunny
When we ventured out together into the snow
We made snowmen and snowballs and hid behind forts
Spending time with each other, for how long, we didn't know.

Time is so precious between young and old
As the clock does not stand still
Moments to treasure between you and I
Our lives, only so much time to fill.

We took a break from our battle and war
To walk hand in hand for a little bit
You run ahead and hide then double back to get me
As your energy I don't have, and I needed to sit.

As I sat on the bench watching you with loving eyes,
A snowflake fell into the palm of my hand
You asked to peer closely at it, to see it in detail
And you marveled at how intricate it was, its shape not bland.

I said, this snowflake is much like you
There is no other one just like it
It is only made once, and when it is ready
Comes to this earth when it sees fit.

It is beautiful and gorgeous just like you
Fine details are what make it unique

And it comes down to bless us with its beauty and awe
For us to enjoy, love but not tweak.

We could never change what a snowflake looks like
But its shape will change form depending on the sun
Like you as time passes us quickly by
Your mind will change shape, your journey begun.

How you change will depend on your weather
Your mood being stormy or warm and bright
Just know that whatever your environment is
Let who you are inside be your guiding light.

You were born perfect and came to this Earth
A perfect soul with so much to learn and grow
I've done my best, as perfect as I could
It was always with love I want you to know.

Take all that I have taught you and go get what you want
Your dreams are yours to seize
They were born from a seed planted a time ago
From a mind that is no longer diseased.

You are perfect exactly the way that you are
Just know your job is to continue to grow
And challenge yourself and break down your barriers
Your limits I hope you will never know.

Surround yourself with like-minded friends
Those who are full of peace and love like you
Share your dreams, your desires your fears
And believe that only good will be coming to you.

I have enjoyed our journey it went by too fast
I learned so much from you
But trust that when you need a hand, advice or ear
My wisdom will once again be there too.

Don't listen to those that do not share your passion
Your dreams and life are yours to go get
Your belief in yourself will carry you through
But never doubt that you aren't perfect.

Only you know what is best for you
I have taught you to be confident and strong
Don't waver in your values and faith
And stay away from lives that don't belong.

You, young girl, are beautiful and bright
Your ability to shine already starting to show
Enjoy your time learning and growing
Endless fields of knowledge are yours to sow.

And when you are ready to pass on all you've learned
Know that there will be plenty girls who will want you
To share your stories, reflections, wins and mistakes
That will make you a wonderful mentor too.

About the Author

Danielle Joworski has masterfully woven elements from the art of writing with helping others learn throughout her career of nearly two decades. However, it wasn't until she made the courageous decision to re-define what balance and family meant that she truly re-connected with childhood passion to write a book to more directly help others achieve their goals. As an adult educator, she appreciates the value in using reflection and story-telling as an experiential method of learning. Through the cathartic process of writing, Danielle shares her personal struggles as well as her triumphant wins over her self-belief in an awe-inspiring manner to relate to both women and young female readers. After earning her Bachelor of Education in Adult Education, she continues on to pursue her passion of helping others to discover their unlimited learning potential by currently completing her Master of Arts in Educational Leadership. A wife and mother of two, Danielle is re-creating her own success story hoping to inspire women to do the same proving that dreams really do come true if you believe in them and believe in yourself.

Made in the USA
Charleston, SC
26 September 2016